WIRED *for* GREATNESS

Spiritual Oxygen

TREVOR R. WALLACE

Outskirts Press, Inc.
http://www.outskirtspress.com

ISBN: 978-1-4787-8779-2

PRINTED IN THE UNITED STATES OF AMERICA

Contents

Who Am I?

Welcome, friends! That is exactly how we want you to feel in the house of God.

Have you ever wondered who you are? We can be identified by many things. Our name, social security number, date of birth, fingerprints, photograph, etc. However, the most important form of ID is to be in Christ. In 2 Corinthians 5:17, it says, "If anyone is in Christ he is a new person. They are not the same any more, for the old life is gone and a new life has begun."

Wow! That is powerful! So now we have new lives to live. We should be giving God the glory with our new lives. If you did not receive his forgiveness and experience this new life, please, I beg you! Don't miss out on your full potential in Christ Jesus. Receive him today. Don't delay.

God bless you all.

Praise the Lord!

Welcome, my friends!

I pray you feel welcome every time you fellowship with us in or out of this sanctuary. Do you know that most people do not praise the Lord? It's a fact. Even some Christians praise the Lord in a very small way. Why is that? Due to lack of knowledge, people don't realize the importance of praising the Lord, the blessing that comes from praising the Lord and, most importantly, the command to praise the Lord. Psalm 150:6 says, "Let everything that has breath praise the Lord!" When Jesus entered Jerusalem in Luke 19:39 and the crowd began praising him, the Pharisees were angry and told Jesus to rebuke the people, but Jesus said to the Pharisees in verse 40 that if the people "keep silent, the rocks will immediately cry out."

So praise the Lord with your lips and your life. Don't be outdone by a rock.

What Are You Thirsty For?

It's no fun being thirsty, so each day we drink water and juice to quench our thirst. That's great for the natural man, but what about the spiritual man? Don't ignore your spiritual thirst, or it will lead to major catastrophes in your life! God invites everyone to partake of His salvation in Isaiah 55:1 when He says, "Is anyone thirsty? Come and drink—even if you have no money! Come, take your choice of wine or milk—it's all free!" The Lord Jesus Christ simplified this invitation and became the mediator between God and man.

So what's the catch, you might ask. Here it is: discipline! We need to discipline ourselves to engage in daily Bible reading, prayer time, and discussion of the Word with someone. This kind of discipline will show God that we are thirsty for His righteousness. We then can start enjoying the eternal life within us since accepting Jesus as our savior. Be thirsty for God and in doing His will. He will always quench your thirst.

God bless you!

You Are in the Light

Light towers are elevated above sea levels to search out watercrafts that are in need of assistance. The light must be high above, or it will be ineffective in reaching miles away. We have a light tower on high that is somewhat similar to that which is used at the seashore. The difference is that the light tower watching us never turns off and always monitors the spirit of mankind.

Proverbs 20:27 (NLT) tells us that "the Lord's light penetrates the human spirit, exposing every hidden motive." That's fine for the person walking upright, but for the person with evil intentions, it's a fright! Let's keep in mind that we are always in God's light. He sees everything, so let's give Him something good to look at. The enemy of our soul, Satan, is lord of darkness, and anyone who loves his ways is his disciple. Jesus Christ is the light of the world, and anyone who loves His ways is His disciple. Allow Jesus Christ, the light of the world, to clean you up so when God the Father penetrates your spirit, your motives will be pleasing to Him.

God bless you!

Believe When You Pray

Some people are merely "top soil" Christians. They don't really believe God will answer their prayers. Have you ever felt that way? First of all, let's establish one thing: God hears all prayers—only His answering our request exactly as requested depends on the question. Let's say an individual is walking upright and makes a request to God that will bring Him glory, that prayer will be answered in God's timing. If the opposite were true—an individual living for himself or herself and not for God—then they should not expect a prayer that will glorify his or her own self to be answered.

David says it best in Psalm 17:5–6: "My steps have stayed on your path; I have not wavered from following you. I am praying to you because I know you will answer, O God. Bend down and listen as I pray." As children of God Most High, we can go boldly to the throne of grace and talk to our heavenly dad! Believe when you pray that God will answer in Jesus's name. If your doubt has kept you "top soil," why not get properly rooted today? Confess to Jesus and believe when you pray because He showed us that He is the way! God bless you!

Catastrophe: A True Eye-Opener

When things appear to be well, most people go along their merry way feeling that there is no need to follow the righteous path. Just as the children of Israel did in times past, we often forget the miracles God performed in our lives—surviving that car accident or surgery, that successful airline flight, saving our marriage, just to name a few.

When we forget the Lord Almighty, He, at times, allows us to undergo major catastrophe. Based on the Word of God, America is in such a state where we ignore true worship and embrace worship of false gods. However, after the catastrophes that Israel faced, they repented and turned from their evil ways. Isaiah Chapter 17:7–8 say, "Then at last the people will look to their Creator and turn their eyes to the Holy One of Israel. They will no longer look to their idols for help or worship what their own hands have made." We, as a nation, can do the same. Now is the time to look to Jesus! If your eyes are clouded, wash them out with the scriptures! Just take a look at the mess around you; only faith in Jesus Christ can give us any real guarantee. The signs are there to see; just open your eyes.

God bless you!

How Do You Praise God?

There are many ways in which we should praise the Lord. We should praise Him in our conversations not only with Christians but also with non-Christians. What if they talk about you or say you are weird? Just so you know, people talk about you anyway, so why not give them something good to talk about? Consider this: if we fail to praise God in our conversations, won't we appear weird in God's eyes? We cannot please everyone, but it's wise to please God.

The most popular method of praise is singing and clapping our hands. Psalm Chapter 47:1 says, "Come, everyone! Clap your hands! Shout to God with joyful praise!" Keep the praise going even after you leave church. Tune in to Christian radio, play Gospel music, and sing along. Allow your praise and worship to chase the demons out of your surroundings while making room for angels. God loves our praise and looks forward to it on a daily basis! Send your praise forth daily—multiple times daily—clap your hands, and sing songs with a smile on your face so the world can see the richness of Christ in you. The many ways you choose to praise God will all be beneficial to you.

God bless you!

It's All Well

Situations may cause you to fall down for a little while, or maybe even a long time, but I encourage you to stay focused on Jesus! Remember, it is during the tough times we get stronger and learn life lessons for the future. Whenever you are faced with a trying situation, call on Jesus and, by faith, believe it's all well.

In 2 Kings 4:23, "It will be all right" was the Shunemite woman's response after realizing that her son had died. The reason she knew it was simply because she had seen the power of God displayed through Elisha, the man of God.

All of us try to figure out why we undergo tough times. Let me help shed some light about it. We undergo tough times so that God's power can be displayed, and He gets the glory. However, some people fail to honor the miracle-working God, believing the problem was solved by the work of their own hands. Don't fall into that category and don't stress yourself when things don't look well. Have faith in Jesus Christ, obey his words, and then say, "It's all well!"

God bless you!

Prepare to Go Out

The church of Jesus Christ is under tremendous attack by Satan and his disciples. We need to be wise in these days and recognize the wolves in our midst. Jesus said it best in Matthew 10:16 (NLT): "Look, I am sending you out as sheep among wolves. So be as shrewd as snakes and harmless as doves." Friends, coworkers, and others we come in contact with will either enhance spiritual growth or subtract from it.

Before leaving your home on a rainy day, you might wear a raincoat, water-friendly footwear or, bare minimum, bring an umbrella. In addition, please open your spiritual eyes before leaving home. Allow the Holy Spirit to lead you in wisdom. You may be attacked but not defeated! You should be so in love with Jesus that even your enemies will be delivered! Remember: be as harmless as a dove. We are not here to hurt people verbally or physically but to love them with the love of Jesus! We can do all things once we partner with Jesus Christ, our Lord and Savior, so let's get prepared.

God bless you!

Approaching the Kingdom

Many people travel during holidays with family. One popular vacation destination is the United Kingdom. A tour of Buckingham Palace is a real treat!

While visiting kingdoms and palaces can be fun, we need to keep the Kingdom of God in clear view! We must be ready in and out of season in order to approach the Kingdom of God. Jesus says this in Mark 1:15: "The time promised by God has come at last! The Kingdom of God is near! Repent of your sins and believe the good news."

If you think you have no sin, think again! We all sin and fall short of God's glory. With that said, let's do as Jesus instructs and repent of our sins. In doing so, we can approach the Kingdom of God with the utmost confidence. Jesus is eternal life and ruler in the physical Kingdom of God. Draw close to Him now to begin to enjoy the spiritual Kingdom of God.

God bless you!

Wise Counsel

"Show me your friends, and I'll tell you who you are." I grew up hearing that phrase and, quite honestly, I believe it's true. Our friends influence us directly or indirectly that we don't even realize that they are rubbing off on us.

We often discuss things with friends and receive counsel in various areas. That could be good or bad depending on the friend. It's bad to receive counsel from friends who are not Christ-centered, for then the counsel is without wisdom. The world cannot give wisdom. Wisdom comes straight from God, so don't accept counsel from the world! It is better to take counsel from a friend connected to Christ and who uses the Word of God as the platform.

Proverbs 13:14 (NLT) states, "The instruction of the wise is like a life-giving fountain; those who accept it avoid the snares of death." I don't know what you are going through right now, but I know the devil will send his disciples to make things worse in your life. Connect with Jesus Christ for yourself so that you can see with spiritual eyes who is wise and who is foolish! Accepting counsel from the wise is the way to go.

God bless you!

The Good Doctor

Most people will consult a doctor for medical assistance when under the weather for a period of time without healing. We, who may very well be healthy physically, might need the emergency room spiritually. The good news is that the doctor is in! He is not on the golf course or on a trip overseas! We can call on Jesus, and He will take care of our needs and, more importantly, grant us His salvation.

Jesus says in Luke Chapter 5:31–32, "Healthy people don't need a doctor—sick people do. I have come to call not those who think they are righteous, but those who know they are sinners and need to repent." Be careful in thinking that you are more righteous than you are. Consult Dr. Jesus and ask Him to reveal your sinful ways. Don't allow the devil to persuade you to leave the emergency room without a heart transformation. The "emergency room"—the church, your prayer closet—should be visited often to get your clean bill of spiritual health from The Good Doctor.

God bless you!

Don't Perish—Flourish!

There is a line that separates success from failure. It comes with instructions to succeed or the choice to fail. That works both naturally and spiritually for small things and great things alike. However, in the spiritual realm of things, failure to follow instructions can cause one to perish or to be destroyed totally, and not just the individual but also the offspring of the individual! In Hosea 4:6, God says, "My people are being destroyed because they don't know me...I refuse to recognize you as my priests. Since you have forgotten the laws of your God, I will forget to bless your children." It sounds serious.

How many times do we neglect God's laws and do our own thing? If we stay on our own path, we will perish. Let's turn from that path, be obedient to the laws of God, love Him with our whole heart, mind, soul and strength, and love our neighbors as ourselves! Do it not just for you but also for your family so they too will receive a blessing. It is time for the church to flourish. Start following God's instructions, and you will be glad you did.

God bless you!

Why Deny?

Christians deny Christ daily without even realizing it. Each time there is an opportunity to help someone out of a jam and we turn a blind eye, we deny Christ. Each time we should lovingly correct a friend or a loved one about lying, cursing, stealing, fornicating, or anger issues and we opt to stay mute, we deny Christ.

In Mark 14:29–30, Peter said to Jesus, "'Even if everyone else deserts you, I never will.' Jesus replied, 'I tell you the truth, Peter—this very night, before the rooster crows twice you will deny three times that you even know me.'"

Jesus knows the fear that we as humans hold on to—fear of being called a Jesus Freak. Newsflash: if we continue denying Christ, not being bold about our beliefs and letting the world know we are changed, God may view us as a Satan Freak. So don't worry what the world may say. Be concerned about what God is saying! After all, God is the one supplying all your needs! Generally speaking, the world doesn't care if you live or die, so embrace God and then testify. Don't deny.

God bless you!

Be Blessed in Every Way

We all undergo life struggles, trials, and tribulation, but even in the midst of it all, God is still on the throne, and He allows us to go through them. Perhaps, it is all part of our testing. Our job is to continue living for God through His son, Jesus Christ, in all that we do so we can be blessed in every way. Once we pass the test, we will be greatly blessed. Abraham underwent a serious test in Genesis 22 when he was asked to sacrifice his son, Isaac. He passed the test, and it was counted unto him as righteousness. Toward the end of his life, the Bible tells us in Genesis 24:1, "Abraham was now a very old man, and the Lord had blessed Him in every way."

We cannot even imagine the type of blessing Abraham received by being a friend of God. Is God your closest and best friend? Do you praise God in the valleys of your life, or are you too busy complaining? It is time to follow our biblical forefathers so that we may achieve the same good results as they did. The scripture works, but we must obey if we desire to be blessed in every way.

God bless you!

Control the Way You Live

"Just go with the flow," says the young lady to her girlfriend in an effort to convince her that "everyone's doing it"—living the immoral life.

It's quite sad to see what society has become. The fear of God has diminished. People live to please themselves rather than to please God. Let me encourage you today to take control of how you live and make it holy. Anyone refusing to take this advice will be controlled by sin. The Bible says in Romans 6:12–13, "Do not let sin control the way you live; do not give in to sinful desires. Do not let any part of your body become an instrument of evil to serve sin. Instead, give yourselves completely to God, for you were dead, but now you have new life. So use your whole body as an instrument to do what is right for the glory of God."

If you know in your heart that you need to be saved, please don't delay. You don't know how much time you have on earth. Confess your sins today. Invite Jesus into your life. He will give you the strength you need to control the way you live. If you are already saved, you have the power within you to say no and walk away from sin, causing the devil to lose and you to win.

God bless you!

So You Think You Are Wise?

Wisdom has been associated with so many insignificant things. For instance, someone may think they are wise because they know how to drive a car. Having the knowledge to operate machinery or put a business together is not what God considers wisdom.

The Bible says in Psalm 14:2, "The Lord looks down from Heaven on the entire human race; He looks to see if anyone is truly wise, if anyone seeks God." So there you have it. If you are not seeking God daily, you are not truly wise. It doesn't matter how many degrees you might have. The Bible says the wisdom of this world is foolishness to God.

Be sure to acquire wisdom from God. Seek Him and His will for your life daily. The Lord Jesus Christ died so we can live for Him. He could have stayed in heaven and watched us perish, but he chose not to. He came and showed us how to live to gain wisdom from God by seeking Him daily. My prayer for you, my friends, is that you will be filled with God's wisdom so that you will prosper spiritually. Everything else is secondary.

God bless you!

A Picture of Love

"For God so loved the world He gave us His only begotten Son" (John 3:16). Those who are wise will accept God's gift of love, repent, turn from their evil ways, and save their souls. The Father's love for His creation is evident each day; just take a look around.

Let's talk about the ocean, for example. Sometimes, it is peaceful and calm; other times, the waves are really high. God loves the beginner swimmer as well as the experienced surfer. The ocean knows exactly where to stop because the Lord controls it. If it weren't for His love—yes, even for this evil world—He could easily send tsunamis similar to the one who killed over one hundred thousand in 2004.

In 1 Corinthians 13:4, it tells us that "love is patient and kind." Isn't that the truth? If you are not doing what you know God desires for you to do, my friend, please stop disappointing the one who loves you the most. Remember to mirror God by being patient with and kind to others. Let them see the love of the Father and our Lord and Savior, Jesus Christ, in you. Allow your lifestyle to become a picture of love.

God bless you!

Simply Wonderful

When looking back at wonderful experiences of the past, they give us smiley faces. We remember graduations from elementary school through college, times we were promoted on jobs, wedding days—just to name a few. I would like to remind you today of the time you needed direction and you sought the Lord's counsel. I know in my life what a wonderful counselor He was, currently is, and always will be. Isaiah 9:6 says, "For a child is born to us, a son is given to us. The government will rest on His shoulders. And He will be called: Wonderful Counselor, Mighty God, Everlasting Father, Prince of Peace."

If you have never sought the Lord in His written Word for counsel, let me encourage you to start today. It is just wonderful! His spirit will speak to you, and you will begin to hear Him more clearly. Don't ignore the counsel of your creator. He wants to grant you joy and peace like never before. Out of all the wonderful events that happen in your life, time spent for Christ is the most wonderful.

God bless you!

God of the Living

Many people don't believe there is life after death. I've heard many times that when you die, that's it for you. On the contrary, when someone dies, it's the start of a whole new life. This new life will be a spiritual life or a spiritual death; however, everyone will be conscious and know where it is they end up.

Jesus had this to say in Luke 20:37–38: "But now, as to whether the dead will be raised—even Moses proved this when he wrote about the burning bush. Long after Abraham, Isaac, and Jacob had died, he referred to the Lord as the God of Abraham, the God of Isaac and the God of Jacob. So he is the God of the living, not the dead, for they are all alive to Him."

So we can best believe that anyone who passed on after living a faith-filled life in Jesus Christ is now with the God of the Living. If you are not born again, you are still dead because you were born into sin. Please turn that around today and start living spiritually. Confess your sins, accept Jesus into your life, and then say with confidence, "I will spend eternity with the God of the living, not the God of the dead!"

God bless you!

Say What?

Words are often spoken without the sufficient thought process needed before speaking—for example, a mother calling her child an idiot or telling him or her, "You'll never be anyone good in life." It goes further than that.

Within the body of Christ, one would think our behavior should differ from that of the world. Not so in many cases. Say what? Don't you realize that our Heavenly Father hears everything we say, sees everything we do, and will judge us accordingly? James 2:12–13 says, "So whatever you say or whatever you do, remember that you will be judged by the law that sets you free. There will be no mercy for those who have not shown mercy to others. But if you have been merciful, God will be merciful when he judges you."

If you are a follower of Christ, don't hide behind the church walls and murder people with your words. God is listening to you. If you are not saved, avoiding verbal murdering will bring you one step closer to salvation. Invite Jesus Christ to take your hand and lead you to the Promised Land. Say what? Yes, the Promised Land, a place far better than we could ever lead ourselves to. Monitor what you say and do. It will bless God and you.

God bless you!

Insight for Living

Ever since creation, breaking the law came with a penalty of some sort, and keeping the law came with rewards. Initially, the laws of God were feared, and most people tried to obey them. What a big difference a few thousand years make! Now, it is the opposite.

The majority of people don't fear God or His commandments. Ironically, people obey traffic laws (at least, most of the time) but ignore God's laws. No wonder there's so much chaos in the world. Remember what the Bible tells us in Psalm 19:8: "Commandments of the Lord are right bringing joy to the heart. The commands of the Lord are clear, giving insight for living." First, we must ask our Heavenly Father for the strength to obey His commandments to the best of our ability. Second, we should listen daily for his supernatural, personalized commands with insight for a great life. No relationship we've established can ever top that. Let's face it: We have all tried to find the right insight for living and failed. The only thing that never failed anyone is a right relationship with God the Father and His son, Jesus Christ. He promises joy to the heart and direction down the right path. Don't follow your heart. Follow Jesus, and He will give you the right insight.

God bless you!

How's Your Faith?

Faith is the confidence that what we hope for will actually happen. It gives us assurance with regard to things we cannot see. So, how's your faith? This is a question each person needs to ask himself.

Let's say someone's faith is small, not believing the Word of God in its entirety nor living it. God won't do great things with that person. On the opposite side, when someone has great faith, great things can happen. The disciples were amazed when a fig tree withered at Jesus's command. Jesus explained to them that they could do the same. Matthew 21:21 (NLT) says, "Then Jesus told them, 'I tell you the truth, if you have faith and don't doubt, you can do things like this and much more. You can even say to this mountain, "May you be lifted up and thrown into the sea," and it will happen.'"

We all have mountains in our lives that can be removed by faith in Jesus Christ. Let's start rebuking anger, poverty, lying or cursive tongue, negative thoughts, and everything else undesirable in our lives. All it takes is faith to believe God will do it for you. Your faith will grow the more you hear God's Word—the Good News—and the more you read the Bible and fellowship with true believers. Increase your faith, my friends, and watch God remove the mountains in your life.

God bless you!

Listen and Obey

We all love when things are pleasing to us—a good meal, a movie, a play, a church service, our relationships with friends and family. Our Heavenly Father also has a desire to be pleased by his creation. During your daily activities, please keep this in mind: everything we say and everything we do will either please God or displease Him. How we tell the difference is simple. Do our actions compliment the Word of God? Are we obedient to His word? Obedience pleases God.

King Saul, the first king of Israel, failed in this area, and the prophet Samuel said to him in 1 Samuel 15:22 (NLT), "What is more pleasing to the Lord: your burnt offerings and sacrifices or your obedience to His voice? Listen! Obedience is better than sacrifice, and submission is better than the fat of rams." Obeying God's Word is the way to go, but how can we obey what we don't know? We need to hear the spoken Word and read it for ourselves. This builds our faith and motivates us to live holy lives! That is what's pleasing to God, and His rewards will always be pleasing to us. Let's begin to listen and obey.

God bless you!

The Ultimate Blessing

Not only are we blessed to be alive, but we are also blessed to be able to read these encouraging words. However, do you know what the ultimate blessing will be? Let's take a look at it in Psalm 24:3–6 (NLT). It says, "Who may climb the mountain of the Lord? Who may stand in His holy place? Only those whose hands and hearts are pure, who do not worship idols and never tell lies. They will receive the Lord's blessing and have a right relationship with God their savior. Such people may seek you and worship in your presence, O God of Jacob."

So, as you see from the scriptures, the ultimate blessing will be standing in God's Holy Place worshipping Him face-to-face. Take the requirements seriously. Keep your heart and hands pure. Don't worship money, relationships, houses, cars, jewelry, sex, or any other idol. Never tell lies. If you were a liar before from this day forward with Jesus Christ's help, get that lying, demonic spirit out of your life. God will bless you here on earth with much more than you deserve if you live to honor Him. These blessings will be just a small taste until the ultimate blessing when you see Him in his Holy Place.

God bless you!

The Holy Spirit Confirms Salvation

Many people ask me, "How do you really know you are saved and are on your way to heaven?" My reply is simply this: the Holy Spirit is leading my life. He is the one that gives me constant peace or a withdrawal of His peace should something need to be fixed within me. Maybe you publicly confessed Jesus Christ and were even water baptized, but that is only the beginning of God's salvation plan. The most challenging part is accepting His will for your life daily (not once a week) by allowing the Holy Spirit to lead you. When you allow Him to take charge, you will experience His love like never before, and you can be sure that you are going to heaven. The Holy Spirit is the only one who knows the way to heaven. Without Him, you are lost.

Romans 5:4–5 (NLT) says, "And endurance develops strength of character, and character strengthens our confident hope of salvation. And this hope will not lead to disappointment. For we know how dearly God loves us, because He has given us the Holy Spirit to fill our hearts with His love." So with that said, please pray to God the Father in the mighty name of Jesus to reveal to you what needs to be fixed in your life. Then ask Him to help you fix it. Eternity is a long time, my friends, so invite the Holy Spirit in your life and keep Him eternally. The other option is eternal death without God's spirit. Be wise.

God bless you!

Be Forgiving to the Dead and the Living

One day, I was asked to rush over to a local hospital to pray for a woman I knew. She had cancer, and the doctors said she only had days to live. The Holy Spirit had me encourage her to forgive her deceased mother of all the wrongs she had done to her. The woman replied, "No, I will not. She can rot in hell!" My heart broke, but I lovingly told her that if she didn't forgive, our Heavenly Father would not forgive her. She still refused. She died five days later without salvation.

Unforgiveness can fester so much hatred that not even death can satisfy. Let's start forgiving others instantly. Matthew 18:21–22 (NLT) says, "Then Peter came to Him and asked, 'Lord, how often should I forgive someone who sins against me? Seven times?' 'No, not seven times,' Jesus replied, 'but seventy times seven!'" The apostles didn't quite understand forgiveness. It's a good thing Peter asked.

We have no excuse. We have the Word of God as our guide. We can see what it says about forgiveness. If you are struggling with unforgiveness, please pray, fast, seek counseling—whatever you can to get rid of it in Jesus's name. If you don't, the Book of Life will not have your name.

God bless you!

Hold On to Your Joy

Many people search for joy but only end up with momentary happiness, the reason being this: joy comes from God, not from the things of this world. Happiness occurs when things of a happy nature happen to us. However, joy should never leave us no matter what happens to us. Nehemiah encouraged the weeping Israelites with regard to this matter. He said in chapter 8, verse 10, "Go and celebrate with a feast of rich foods and sweet drinks, and share gifts of food with people who have nothing prepared. This is a sacred day before our Lord. Don't be dejected and sad, for the joy of the Lord is your strength!"

My friends, today is a day the Lord has made. Hold on to your joy in Him! If, for some reason, you don't have joy, first get the one who gives joy freely by accepting Jesus Christ as Lord and Savior. Then, live in that joy, and it will surely strengthen you. Don't watch the circumstances you may be in. Keep your eyes on Jesus, the one who is bigger than your circumstance.

Treat yourself and someone less fortunate to a meal. Celebrate Jesus and the joy He gives, which strengthens us. Hold on to your joy—it's your choice.

God bless you!

Your True Identity

When traveling by commercial airline, we have to check in at the counter. The first thing you're usually asked to do is to identify yourself by way of driver's license, passport, or other ID. While these forms of identification are good for the world's order system, they are not our true identity. This is not to say that we carry false documents (although some do), but what I am saying is that our true identity is based on how God sees us. When God looks at us, He sees a believer or a nonbeliever.

The Bible says this in Ephesians 3:6 (NLT): "And this is God's plan: Both Gentiles and Jews who believe the Good News share equally in the riches inherited by God's children. Both are part of the same body, and both enjoy the promise of blessings because they belong to Christ Jesus." So, let's identify ourselves to God as believers by the way we live in love, by testifying about His goodness, by being forgiving, by showing mercy, and so on! This is not a lip service thing. If you are a Jew or a Gentile living without Christ, then you are a nonbeliever.

Let's change that today by accepting Jesus Christ as Lord and leader of your life. After that, my friend, you can rejoice because your identity will be a believer in the Good News of Jesus Christ. Heaven will be awaiting you. The devil will try to win you back, but God will give you the strength to resist him. So, spiritually identify yourself.

God bless you!

A Cry for Help

We as a people cry for many different reasons. One cry that is dear to my heart is when an individual seeks help from the Lord and it seems He is nowhere to be found. I want you to know He is right there listening to your every prayer and will help in His perfect timing.

In Psalm 22:1 (NLT), David prophesied what Jesus would say on the cross: "My God, my God, why have you abandoned me? Why are you so far away when I groan for help?" Jesus said these very words when the spirit of God the Father withdrew from Him. You see, on the cross, Jesus took on all the sins of the world, so the Father had to leave Him. Sin is ugly to God; it cannot be in His presence. Many of us cry out for help; however, we should confess the sin in our lives first. After we confess, the Holy Spirit will draw close to us again and take us though our ordeals with great peace. I am not saying you won't have trying times, but what I am saying is you will make it through the trying times victoriously.

So ask the Lord to point out the problematic areas in your life. Confess them and pray for all the help you desire, and He will help you.

God bless you!

Write It on Your Heart

Out of the many things written on our hearts, some come to mind regularly; for instance, "For God so loved the world that He gave His only Son, so that everyone who believes in Him will not perish but have eternal life" (John 3:16, NLT). Some choose to remember that scripture and figure, "I can sin all I want. Since I believe in Jesus, I will make it to heaven."

Let me lovingly give you another scripture to write on your hearts: 2 Timothy 2:19 says, "But God's truth stands firm like a foundation stone with this inscription: 'The Lord knows those who are His,' and 'All who belong to the Lord must turn away from evil'" (NLT).

Please put away evil, my friends. Accept Jesus Christ as Lord and do His will. You will then have a personal relationship with Jesus Christ. Many would say, "I know about Jesus," but rarely do we hear someone say, "Jesus knows I belong to Him!" Let's write these scriptures on our hearts and stay prepared for heaven because soon we will depart.

God bless you!

Why Can't We All Just Get Along?

If you are sick and tired of hatred, prejudice, racism, wars, crime, and violence, well, I feel the same way you do. For some odd reason, harmony is not a top priority in the world today. Can you imagine what our lives would be like if we all just got along? Wow, it would be amazing!

David says in Psalm 133:1–3 (NLT), "How wonderful and pleasant it is when brothers live together in harmony! For harmony is as precious as the anointing oil that was poured over Aaron's head, that ran down his beard and onto the border of his robe. Harmony is as refreshing as the dew from Mount Hermon that falls on the mountains of Zion. And there the Lord has pronounced His blessing, even life everlasting." Nations, cities, families, and individuals are missing God's blessings because they lack harmony. We can't change the entire world, but we can change our world by living in harmony with those around us. In doing so, we will reap the rewards that accompany harmonious living. The time when everyone will live in harmony will not be in effect until we reach heaven, and I can hardly wait for that day!

Be sure to secure your reservation, my friends. Only a personal relationship with Jesus Christ can get us there. Should you decide to accept Him, or if you already have, do His will daily and leave the rest to Him. Through Him, we can live in harmony.

God bless you!

You Are Not a Frog

"Sometimes you feel like a nut; sometimes you don't," was the famous Mars bar slogan. Unfortunately, many church parishioners sing the song, "Sometimes you feel like a Christian; sometimes you don't."

Someone once said to me—and I quote, "I have tried the church thing, and it just didn't work for me." These are often people who hop from place to place trying to find joy and peace. The first sign of hardship sparks another leap. In 1 Peter 4:1–2, it says, "So then, since Christ suffered physical pain, you must arm yourselves with the same attitude He had, and be ready to suffer, too. For if you have suffered physically for Christ, you have finished with sin."

Whether you're suffering results from a relationship, financial issues, or sickness in your body, Jesus is aware and right there to see you through. You are not a frog, so there is no need to hop away from His will. Don't go with the flows; go with Jesus wherever He takes you. Job and relationship-hopping may be severe, but hopping away from Jesus Christ will result in a nightmare. Hang in there, and He will see you through.

God bless you!

Who Do You Follow?

We've all looked to someone as a role model. For many, it was Mom or Dad, a teacher, a business leader, a TV or movie star, a friend, or a pastor. While admiring the attributes of these personnel is great, we need to focus on whom we should really follow. The answer is Jesus!

The early church in Corinth didn't quite understand this, so they idolized their teachers in the Gospel. In 1 Corinthians 3:4–5, the apostle Paul corrected them when he said, "When one of you says, 'I am a follower of Paul,' and another says, 'I follow Apollos,' aren't you acting just like people of the world? After all, who is Apollos? Who is Paul? We are only God's servants through whom you believed the Good News." On the other hand, Jesus said this in Matthew 4:19 when recruiting His first disciples: "Come, follow me, and I will show you how to fish for people!"

Note with me what following Jesus entails. It is a mandate to reach out to lost souls for Him. Don't waste precious energy trying to imitate someone other than Jesus. Get connected to the real superhero, conqueror, star, awesome one, role model, Savior Jesus Christ. Follow Him in leading others to salvation. Some talk a good talk, but I encourage you, my friends, to walk the walk and make Jesus proud. He is the only one who will never lead you astray.

God bless you!

Who Are You Mocking?

As a young boy, I used to play a game called Monkey Face. Others probably played the same game, maybe with a different name. The object is simply making faces at someone, mocking them in a victorious manner—for example, "I am right, and you are wrong! Naa naa naa naa naaa!"

Believe it or not, people still play that game in their adult lives. However, they should be careful their faces don't freeze in that position. On a more serious note, people often mock God with their double standard lifestyles. How foolish can they be? The Bible says in Galatians 6:7, "Don't be misled—you cannot mock the justice of God. You will always harvest what you plant."

There you have it, my friends. Whatever we plant in secret or openly, God sees it, and that is what we shall reap. Anyone trying to pull a fast one on God is actually mocking themselves. So don't be slick in your walk with God. Give Him your whole heart, mind, soul, and body, and He will give you a whole lot more in return. Leave the monkey faces to the monkeys.

God bless you!

A Glimpse of the Glory

When in conversation, we hear the words "Jesus," "The Messiah," "The Lamb of God," etc., and we may instantly get a picture in our minds of what He might look like. The prophet Ezekiel got a glimpse of His glory, and this is how he described Him in Ezekiel 1:27–28: "From what appeared to be His waist up, He looked like gleaming amber, flickering like a fire. And from His waist down, He looked like a burning flame, shining with splendor. All around Him was a glowing halo, like a rainbow shining in the clouds on a rainy day. This is what the glory of the Lord looked like to me."

Amazing! Now comes the challenge: are you ready to see the glory in a favorable manner? So many are not living for Jesus, although deep in their hearts there is a lot of good. Unfortunately, "good people" don't qualify to live with Christ. *God* people do.

To see His Glory without fear and trembling, get to know Him starting today. We will meet Him as a friend or as a judge, so let me encourage you to become His friend. Don't be like the many who have gone on before us and regretfully said, "If only I knew!" Now that you know, why get a glimpse of His glory when you can live in it?

God bless you!

Talk About Jesus

The best promotion has been and always will be word of mouth. Information circulates very fast when people start talking, so be careful what you talk about. Make sure your words are for building the kingdom of God. Jesus should be the one whom we talk about most because a relationship with Him is most important. During His teaching ministry among men, everyone was talking about Jesus. Mark 6:14 (NLT) says, "Herod Antipas, the king, soon heard about Jesus, because everyone was talking about Him."

While that is amazing to me, it then saddens me that so many these days are talking about everything else but not about Jesus. Just a reminder: we were *created* and created to worship God the Father and our Lord Jesus Christ. This leads me to conclude that the evolutionist who believes we evolved from monkeys has things backward. However, the very fact that we fail to talk about Jesus as we should does proves that we have strayed from what we were created for.

Let's not imitate the monkey and ignore our giving honor to Jesus. Ignoring Jesus confirms our minds have deteriorated, and we are less than the human beings we were created to be. Start talking about Jesus and stop monkeying around.

God bless you!

The Ultimate Protection

Most people consider their own protection a top priority. They install alarm systems in their homes, security cameras, energized fences; some even buy firearms for protection. All these measures of protection are still not foolproof; there is always a way around them. Let me encourage you to seek the ultimate protection. He is the Lord Jesus Christ!

David says in Psalm 11:1 (NLT), "I trust in the Lord for protection. So why do you say to me, 'Fly like a bird to the mountains for safety!'" David's friends encouraged him to run from his enemies. However, there is no need to flee from our situations, trials, or enemies if we have the ultimate protector watching out for us

Not everyone has signed up for this package though. If you haven't done so, please don't delay any longer. Now is the time to accept Jesus Christ as Lord and Savior. Don't rely on man-made protection that will fail. Trust in the Lord who never fails. He sees what's around every corner and will have his people proceed forward, stop, or go another route. He will fight our battles for us so we can experience a greater level of peace and joy. Have I mentioned that this package is priceless and that it costs you nothing out of pocket? What a great deal! Sign up today. He is available.

God bless you!

How Many Times Must He Call?

We all may have heard the phrase, "stubborn as a mule," but honestly speaking, humans are far more stubborn than mules. How many people do we know, ourselves included, who ignore God's calling on our lives? We know what we should do but choose not to do it for various reasons. We don't know how many times God will call, so please answer His call immediately.

The young prophet, Samuel, went through this process, and this is what the Bible says in 1 Samuel 3:8–9: "So the Lord called a third time, and once more Samuel got up and went to Eli. 'Here I am. Did you call me?' Then Eli realized it was the Lord who was calling the boy. So he said to Samuel, 'Go lie down again, and if someone calls again, say, "Speak, Lord, your servant is listening."' So Samuel went back to bed."

Like Samuel, most people don't recognize the voice of the Lord. If that's your situation, establish a marriage relationship with Jesus. He is the bridegroom who will be returning for His church, the bride. It is wise to know him for yourself and relate to Him daily as one would do in a natural marriage relationship. When our wives or husbands call, we answer the phone, don't we? Let's answer the call from heaven. Salvation awaits, along with His joy and peace.

God bless you!

Are You Following His Teaching?

There are pastors, bishops, apostles and the like teaching millions of God's people around the world on a weekly basis. While this is a good thing, we have a severe problem with some congregants and teachers. They suffer from the "refusal to follow" syndrome. While it is refreshing to hear a word taught in a comfy environment, what good is it if we don't follow?

Jesus says in Matthew 7:24 (NLT), "Anyone who listens to my teaching and follows it is wise, like a person who builds a house on solid rock." The intelligent person quickly realizes that if we are not living according to God's Word, we are not wise. God is not impressed by how many degrees you may have acquired through the years. True wisdom comes from God and not the world.

Study His teachings on your own and in a good Bible-teaching church. Learn His ways and then live them. Following the teachings of Jesus will not only bring you blessings on earth but also eternal living with the King.

God bless you!

Your Dreams Can Come True

Many people live, have great dreams, and die without seeing them come true. Do you know that there is a simple explanation for that? Before we continue, let's look at what the Bible says in Proverbs 13:19: "It is pleasant to see dreams come true, but fools refuse to turn from evil to attain them."

This leads me to conclude that we are directly responsible for our dreams becoming a reality. The first thing we must do is establish a right working relationship with Jesus Christ, and then we can hear His voice clearly. Our dreams that line up with His will can come true, but if we are practicing evil, we can forget it. Evil is more than the obvious lying, stealing, or killing. Evil is not honoring God in our conversations, henceforth, giving Satan the glory. Evil is failure to give God the credit and the glory in all the circumstances we face. The Bible says we are fools if we embrace evil and watch our dreams pass us by or fade away.

Let's turn things around starting today. Pray to the Lord of great dreams and ask him to establish you by writing your name in the Heaven's Lamb's Book of Life. Dream great dreams and watch them come true. Nothing is too hard for us to accomplish with Jesus Christ. But don't take my word for it; taste Him and see for yourself.

God bless you!

Direct Connect

Never underestimate the prayers of the righteous. We, who are made righteous by faith in Jesus Christ, have the ability, the power, and the permission to pray for people. However, the church is failing in this area. We tend to forget that we are the ones with the direct connect. The result is sad. Many who are unclean because of sin die the same way—without repenting.

Let's look at one man's prayer and see the result. In 2 Chronicles 30:18–20, Hezekiah said, "May the Lord, who is good, pardon those who decide to follow the Lord, the God of their ancestors, even though they are not properly cleansed for the ceremony." And the Lord listened to Hezekiah's prayer and healed the people.

Christians, please do remember that none of us are without sin, so stop judging and start praying. Use your direct connection to improve your situation. Ask yourself this question: How many people do I really pray for? I tell you the truth—as the spirit of God leads me to write this, I myself am convicted to pray for more salvations. Don't just connect with God for temporary things. Eternal things are far more beneficial. Pray and watch miracles come your way.

God bless you!

You Will Be Rescued

Lifeguards play a very important role at the beach and at swimming pools. In the event someone is drowning, they are right there to rescue. We sometimes feel as if we are drowning in the troubles of life, but be encouraged—we have a spiritual lifeguard.

David says this in Psalm 34:19: "The righteous person faces many troubles, but the Lord comes to the rescue each time." When we become followers of Jesus Christ, we are entitled to numerous promises. Many people don't live in victory and perish for lack of knowledge. Here is some knowledge: the Lord Jesus Christ is our advocate, our deliverer, and our savior! He will rescue His people from all of life's trials in His perfect timing. Whatever we are drowning in today—marriage issues, financial difficulty, health problems—no challenge is too difficult for Jesus to come to our rescue.

Let's do our part to honor Him, live for Him to the best of our ability, and watch him work while rescuing us. The same Lord who parted the Red Sea and allowed the Israelites to cross over on dry ground will take away our floodwaters and give us solid ground.

God bless you!

You Don't Have to Die

"You don't have to die" will cause some reaction from the reader's heart, I am sure. Some will laugh and say, "Yeah, right." Others will look into it and say, "How much does it cost?" The fountain of youth has been sought after for many years now to no avail. Here is the secret, so, reader, please pay attention.

Those who are born-again believers with a right relationship with God will never die. Even if they have said good-bye to this earthly location, they are very much alive in heaven, speaking to Jesus there. The Bible says this in Hebrews 2:9–10: "Yes, by God's grace, Jesus tasted death for everyone. God, for whom and through whom everything was made, chose to bring many children into glory. And it was only right that he should make Jesus, through His suffering, a perfect leader, fit to bring them into their salvation." In other words, my friends, Jesus died and defeated hell so we don't have to die spiritually or experience hell. His salvation plan is the best, so don't be so focused on your earthly retirement plans! Get connected to the true and living God and our Savior, Jesus Christ, and live with the utmost confidence that death has lost the victory over your soul. You are not qualified to die if Christ is leading your life. He already tasted death for you. Don't taste it for yourself.

God bless you!

Your Will Be Done

Many times in prayer we say things we don't mean. One of the most popular is: "Lord let your will be done." Then, ironically, we ignore the Holy Spirit's lead.

Listen to how David prayed in Psalm 143:10–11: "Teach me to do your will, for you are my God. May your gracious Spirit lead me forward on a firm footing. For the glory of your name, O Lord, preserve my life. Because of your faithfulness, bring me out of this distress."

David realized that his distress stemmed from doing things his own way, and the Holy Spirit needed to lead him in a life of peace. Isn't that the truth many of us can understand oh so well? Start looking for the Holy Spirit's straight and narrow path. It is His will for you to walk on it. Yes, it is easier to walk the broad path, but it is not God's will to see you perish.

Put on the whole armor of God daily before things get hectic so that you may hear the Holy Spirit giving instructions and guiding your path. When praying, "Lord, let your will be done," mean it and accept His will. It may be hard at times, but He will see us through, and, in the end, we will have the victory.

God bless you!

There Is Always Something

Something always pops up. Our days never go 100 percent as planned. There is always something. How do we deal with surprises, bad or good? When obstacles arise, how do we respond?

Let's never forget: we can plan all we want, but God determines what will happen. My advice is to live out Psalm 37:34, which says: "Put your hope in the Lord. Travel steadily along His path. He will honor you by giving you the land." Key point: "Put your hope in the Lord." You can rest assured that He will take care of your every need if you put your hope in Him. The devil will try and destroy your hope with disappointments, losses, heartbreaks, and the like, but don't allow him. Keep the Holy Spirit in front of you, leading the way, with you following on the path of righteousness. With this accomplished, you will inherit the land.

There is always something, but guess what? There is always a friend, a savior, and Lord in Jesus Christ. With Him, you will never be shaken.

God bless you!

Have You Seen The Light?

Imagine a world without light. If we didn't have the sun, moon, stars, electricity, or any light-giving force, what a catastrophe that would be! Although the thought is mind-blowing, remember this: the spiritual man requires more light than the natural man in order to properly function. To prove this fact, interview someone who is visually impaired but who loves Jesus to see how much "light" they have.

Isaiah 9:2 says, "The people who walk in darkness will see a great light. For those who live in a land of deep darkness, a light will shine." The Light of the World has made himself available. The question is: have you seen the Light? Your spirit man will be in darkness, unless you allow the Light to lead. No one wants to continue bumping into harmful obstacles, but that is what will happen without the Light.

My friends, Jesus Christ is the Light you need, who will never leave you nor forsake you and who will keep you from falling. Get to know Him. Turn on the Light by closing your eyes, tune out the things of this world, and allow His spirit to minister to yours. Invite His presence with a sincere heart, and He will come. Get out of darkness.

God bless you!

He Never Changes

Did you ever partake of an activity as an adult that used to be fun as a child but now it's lost its excitement—for instance, playing hopscotch or jump rope? There may be a few adults who still enjoy those things, but most probably will not.

We, as people, change over the years. The things we enjoy change, our goals change, our relationships change, and so on. This led me to wonder if Jesus ever changes. Well, the answer is No. Hebrews 13:8 says, "Jesus Christ is the same yesterday, today, and forever." What keeps Him in line is total dedication to the will of God the Father. His spirit is one with the Father, and He allowed nothing or no one to change that.

We can learn a lot from Him. In a world where change is noted as good, be certain you are not changing for the worse. A good rule of thumb is to ensure you are doing the will of God the Father, and your spirit is one with Him. If we should stray, He will tug at our hearts as a gentle reminder. Listen and turn from sin before it's too late. When Satan tempted Jesus, Jesus said to him, "Get out of here, Satan! You must worship the Lord your God and serve only Him!" Jesus did not change in heaven or on earth, and neither should we who live for God. If you are not saved, please make a change for the better and stay that way.

God bless you!

Who Is Your Inspiration?

Over the years, many people have inspired me to do things—some good things and some bad. After giving my life to Jesus Christ, I made Him my ultimate inspiration. I want to be like Him.

After Jesus, my inspiration is John the Baptist. John was a preacher who told everyone to repent and turn to God. He didn't work miracles, he didn't preach prosperity and building your earthly kingdom, and he never tried to take the glory away from Jesus. To the surprise of many, this is what Jesus said about John in Luke 7:28 (NLT): "I tell you, of all who have ever lived, none is greater than John. Yet even the least person in the Kingdom of God is greater than he is!"

To hear Jesus testify about John inspires me to do the things John did—to tell people Jesus is coming again soon and tell them to repent, which means to tell God you are sorry and that you'll turn from your sinful ways. Each person should choose an inspiration that has eternal value. A few years ago, there was a popular saying: "I want to be like Mike." Let's change that to, "I want to be like Jesus!" Imitate those who imitate Jesus Christ. Your inspiration should be a Christ-led individual.

God bless you!

Primary Care

Everyone loves being cared for. Some have a primary care physician—a family doctor who knows them personally. We can all have a primary care physician, healer, and friend in Jesus. Strangely enough though, most people ignore Him rather than work alongside him. The human mind cannot fully comprehend the sovereignty of God, but for those of us who have an established relationship with Him, we should be humbled by His care for us. David says this in Psalm 8:4 (NLT): "What are mere mortals that you should think about them, human beings that you should care for them?"

Yes, my friends, we are under God's care, even if we don't care for Him. If you have yet to recognize Him for who He is, it is not too late to do so today. When your heart stops beating, it will be too late. Before crossing train tracks, we should stop, look, and listen. Remember, there is a train trying to run you over. The one who dispatched the "demon" train is Satan, the enemy of your soul. Fight back with Jesus as the head of your life, then you can rest assured that your spiritual eyes and ears will be open to see and hear when the enemy is near so that you can defend yourself. Jesus cares for you in many ways, my friend. Let Him into your heart and let your life begin.

God bless you!

Embrace Common Sense

I have heard it said, "Common Sense is not so common." Some claim to be so smart but fail when it comes to having common sense, especially in the spiritual area. The world's standard of common sense is a bit different from what God sees as common sense. While the world's idea of common sense may not be all bad, it lacks the key ingredient, which is a right relationship with God. That is why some well-educated people suffer so much daily, or even commit suicide, for lack of peace.

You see, peace, joy, and a right mind only come from God. Proverbs 3:21–23 say, "My child, don't lose sight of common sense and discernment. Hang on to them, for they will refresh your soul. They are like jewels on a necklace. They keep you safe on your way, and your feet will not stumble."

The utmost common sense in God's eye is to live for Him; everything else is secondary. Take my advice, my friends, and accept Him today. Embrace common sense. Jesus Christ will welcome you with open arms and bless you from then to eternity. Your eyes will be open to see clearly all things you were once blind to. Common sense will be made common when Christ is the center of our lives.

God bless you!

Good! But Is It Good for You?

Many things in life appear to be good—receiving a promotion by way of "just a little" compromise, fatty food and desserts, a relationship that lacks God's blessing. The list goes on and on, but the question is this: are these things good for you? Let's make this personal. In order to determine well, you need the one who is good to guide you. Psalm 136:1 says, "Give thanks to the Lord, for He is good! His faithful love endures forever."

God's faithful love is the definition of mercy, which tells us He is ready and willing to forgive. Accept the one who is good. His Holy Spirit will then guide you. He will point out the bad—people, places, and things—you once thought were good. Don't fight Him and try to hold on to the junk He wants to remove from your life. Just let it go. Some of the bad we embrace is well-decorated and cannot be seen with the natural eye. It is imperative to have the good Lord take the blinders off our eyes so we can see the tricks of the enemy. Always remember: it may taste, look, or feel good, but we shouldn't if God wouldn't.

God bless you!

Help Is on the Way

Many 9-1-1 operators conclude calls of distress by saying, "Help is on the way!" If you or a loved one is sick, it is a comforting feeling to know help is on the way by way of an ambulance. If one were being robbed at gunpoint and the police arrived in time to stop it, well, that's an even better feeling.

David too knew about waiting with the assurance that help was on the way and experiencing God's wonderful help. This is what he says in Psalm 40:1–2: "I waited patiently for the Lord to help me, and He turned to me and heard my cry. He lifted me out of the pit of despair, out of the mud and mire. He set my feet on solid ground and steadied me as I walked along."

Whatever you are going through right now, please remember to trust the Lord Jesus Christ and wait on Him. If your faith remains in Him, I guarantee you that help is on the way. It may come today, tomorrow, or next week—only God knows—but be encouraged, my friends. He will never let you down. His timing is perfect and lines up with His will. All we need to do is be still. Help is on the way.

God bless you!

The Power to Succeed Financially

Most people want to be financially successful—to live life without having to worry about bills, college tuition, or retirement savings. "It sounds great but not realistic," some might say. If that is your mindset, my friend, you need to change it. It is God's desire for us to be financially successful. This is what He says through Moses in Deuteronomy 8:18 (NLT): "Remember the Lord your God. He is the one who gives you power to be successful, in order to fulfill the covenant He confirmed to your ancestors with an oath." Jesus confirms in John 10:10 that He came to give us life more abundantly.

If our finances are a mess, it is difficult to live life abundantly. We need to ensure our covenant with God is intact. Don't break the contract. If we uphold our end of the deal—to live for him totally—He will make us successful. Unlike the world's success, when God increases our wealth, He adds no stress to it. He gives us peace like a river as well as overwhelming joy. Perhaps, you are totally sold out to Jesus yet still struggling financially. If that is you, I have great news. Joy will come in the morning. The storm is about over. God has not forgotten you. Keep the faith and speak blessings over your finances. By your faith, you will touch the heart of God, which is all the power you need to succeed.

God bless you!

Just How Safe Are You?

Some purchase a gun for safety. Others buy a dog or install a security system. Even with these in place, just how safe are you? If the enemy shoots first, your gun is useless. What if the dog is bribed with a piece of steak or someone cracks the code to your security system? These scenarios may never happen, but they very well could.

The Bible says this in Proverbs 18:10–11: "The name of the Lord is a strong fortress; the godly run to Him and are safe. The rich think of their wealth as a strong defense; they imagine it to be a wall of safety." My friends, whether you are rich, poor, or somewhere in-between, be sure to put your trust in the Lord Jesus Christ for your safety. The media will tell you differently, but all you need to know is contained in the Holy Bible.

The Bible is often referred to as a sword, which is what we need to fight our spiritual enemy, the devil. We also need our "sword" to love our human "enemies." This is impossible to accomplish without the spirit of God living in us, directing and protecting us. Protection not only from an enemy but also from our own flesh. Just how safe are you? Very safe when living for Christ.

God bless you!

Nearer Than You Think

Just how near to us is the God of creation? The answer: very near. So near, in fact, that He sees everything we do in public or in private. He also hears everything we say. This is what grabbed me though—He knows everything we think about, and He monitors the intent of our hearts.

For those with a close relationship with Jesus Christ, it's not a problem having the all-seeing eye of God around. On the other hand, for the unsaved, well, they'd rather He weren't looking. Asaph thanked God for being near. This is what he said in Psalm 75:1: "We thank you, O God! We give thanks because you are near. People everywhere tell of your wonderful deeds." Isn't that the truth? In every country, in every race, there is someone proclaiming the name of Jesus! When someone tells me they don't believe in God, I tell them, "He still believes in you."

I don't know about you, but I make it a priority to know the one who is always nearest to me in a friendly way. What does that mean? It means we have another spiritual being lurking around in an unfriendly way. Only when we search the scriptures will the unseen world be revealed. Food for thought: angels and demons are near, much nearer, than you think. Get to know your Creator by studying His Word and singing praise thanksgiving.

God bless you!

Only for a Season

Because it is a fallen world, all things here on Earth must come to an end. Luxurious, average, or inadequate lifestyles will all come to an end. Some of us are persecuted in many ways by evil people. We should pray for our persecutors and ask God to bless them so unforgiveness doesn't have the chance to set in. Hopefully, they will change their ways because if not, terror will grip them. This is what the Bible says in Psalm 14:4–5: "Will those who do evil never learn? They eat up my people like bread and wouldn't think of praying to the Lord. Terror will grip them, for God is with those who obey Him."

Our trials in this life are only for a season, my friends. Keep your eyes on Jesus because soon the trials will all end. Show love, forgiveness, kindness, and patience. Shine your light and remember that whatever the circumstance, it's only for a season. Be encouraged. Verse 5 said, "God is with those who obey Him." You can make it in Jesus's name. If you are one doing evil deeds, stop and change your ways. If you are on the right track, by all means, continue. Soon you will see your King face-to-face.

God bless you!

Matters of Mercy

A man once told me he would not attend my church—or any church, for that matter. I asked him why, and his response was this: God has turned His back on mankind. He continued, referring me to scriptures about God being sorry He created man and how God wiped man from the face of the earth by way of flood. The gentleman then asked, "If God is all-knowing, why didn't He know mankind would sin against Him?"

The answer is this: we all have two roads before us each day. God knows both roads and where they end, but He gives us free will to choose our own way. God has a heart that gets broken when we ignore or deny Him. It's not that he doesn't know. Our poor choices hurt Him. We must choose the road that brings glory to God. The other road brings grief to your Maker. Although sin keeps us away from God, He is still merciful to us when we turn to Him. Psalm 116:5 says, "How kind the Lord is! How good He is! So merciful, this God of ours!" So, this message is for anyone who questions God's mercy.

No matter what you have done in your life, you can confess your sins, and God will forgive you and show you mercy. Turn to Him today and don't delay. God did not stop showing you mercy. You are still alive, aren't you?

God bless you!

Dangerous Influence

It breaks my heart as a pastor to warn Christians about other believers. It is one thing to have the world negatively influence you, but someone in the family of God? It is what I call a dangerous influence. Believers tend to put their guard down a bit when dealing with a brother or sister in the Lord. Please be reminded that the devil also comes into the church looking for an opportunity to strike.

Just remember, when you cause someone to sin, you are sinning against Christ yourself. The apostle Paul says this in 1 Corinthians 8:12: "And when you sin against other believers by encouraging them to do something they believe is wrong, you are sinning against Christ." Whatever negative influence you have been or may still be, I urge you to stop. Jesus said that the person with ears to hear should listen and understand what the Spirit is saying to the churches. If you are not a part of the church, then you have another monkey on your back. Shake off the demonic spirit and accept Jesus Christ today for your salvation. Dangerous influences will keep you from salvation and cause you to surrender your rights to heaven. Be wise in your influencing and who influences you.

God bless you!

Get Up Again

Stumbling blocks are everywhere we turn—in relationships, business dealings, investments. These things fail from time to time and set us back emotionally, financially, and even spiritually. As believers in Christ, we need to remember that we have Jesus looking out for our best interests so we can, by faith, get up again. The Bible says in Proverbs 24:16: "The godly may trip seven times, but they will get up again. But one disaster is enough to overthrow the wicked."

If this life has dealt you a few hard blows that have knocked you down, pray to the Father for strength and get up again. Exercise your faith, my friends. A popular saying goes: "What doesn't cost your life doesn't cost anything." In other words, as long as you are still living, there is hope in Jesus's name. No matter how much or whom you have lost, you can still get up again. We often pray hardest when at our lowest in life. Don't blame God for anything; just cry out to Him because He is king. If you are His child, He promises that you will get up again. If you are not, begin a close and personal relationship with Him today so that His promise will be extended to you as well.

God bless you!

Loving Forever

Songwriters often write lyrics claiming they will love someone forever. When people first fall in love, or when they say their wedding vows, they promise, "It's you and I forever, baby." However, that is a very tall order. Conditions often arise that change the strong feelings we may have once had for each other. Sometimes what was once love turns to hatred. Praise be to God, whose love will truly last forever. Psalm 103:16–18 says, "The wind blows, and we are gone—as though we had never been here. But the love of the Lord remains forever with those who fear Him." His salvation extends to the children's children of those who are faithful to his covenant, of those who obey his commandments.

My friends, be sure to obey the Lord's commands. Only then can we rest assured His love for us will remain forever. I am reminded of the warning sign often posted near a lake or pool, which states: "Swim at your own risk." When we sin, it is at our own risk. My advice to you is for you to get sin out of your life and put on Jesus Christ. When we stand before God as judge, believe me, you want him to show you love him and not say, "Depart from me, I never knew you." Ignorance is never an excuse. The Bible says study to show yourself approved.

God bless you!

Escape the Traps

There are many traps set for people on a daily basis. The police highway patrols set their speed traps, while even shady business personnel set financial traps. However, there is one trap more dangerous of them all—the trap of sin. The Bible says in Proverbs 29:5–6, "To flatter friends is to lay a trap for their feet. Evil people are trapped by sin, but the righteous escape, shouting for joy."

Proverbs 29:6 makes it plain to see whether you are evil or righteous based on your affiliation with sinful activities. My prayer for all who read this encouragement is that you choose the righteous path and escape the traps. The sin in our lives will keep us away from a close relationship with God. The devil can then have his way with us.

Escape the traps of sin today by confessing all your sin to God and asking Jesus to come into your life and show you what to do. If you do that, my friends, then you also will shout for joy as you escape the traps of sin. Don't take this lightly, because the wages of sin is death. But the free gift of God is eternal life through Christ Jesus. Escape the traps today.

God bless you!

The Antidote

If you were poisoned by a cobra, you would need the antidote to save your life. In that scenario, it would be the antivenom.

The world was poisoned by Satan when he influenced Adam and Eve to sin. The power of sin was let loose into the world and has been killing ever since. So, one might ask: what's the antidote for the power of sin? The answer is found in Romans 6:6–7 (NLT): "We know that our old sinful selves were crucified with Christ so that sin might lose its power in our lives. We are no longer slaves to sin. For when we died with Christ we were set free from the power of sin."

The antidote for sin is to surrender your life to Jesus. When the Holy Spirit enters in, He will rearrange things and kick sin to the curb. Don't try to hold on to the things He is throwing out. Adapt to the righteous change and see miracles happen in your life. The best is yet to come when we see Jesus face-to-face as a friend. Get the antidote today so your sins will be washed away. Study the Word, go to church and bible studies—do whatever you can to fight the temptations from the evil one.

God bless you!

Endless Praise

A few things we do with our mouths: eat often, talk (sometimes too much), whistle, and sigh/breathe. However, we must never forget what the Lord wants from us. He has twenty-four elders around Him at all times giving Him praise. Revelation 4:10–11 (NLT) says: "The twenty-four elders fall down and worship the one sitting on the throne (the one who lives forever and ever). And they lay their crowns before the throne and say, 'You are worthy, O Lord our God, to receive glory and honor and power. For you created all things, and they exist because you created what you pleased.'"

We, as humans, were created for praise and worship. Why do you think we are always singing? If you currently only sing in the shower, be encouraged. If you were that bad you would have caused the water to stop running. Begin your endless praise today. David says in Psalm 34:1 (NLT): "I will praise the Lord at all times. I will constantly speak His praises." David knew the value of praise and worship. Don't ever think your praise is going unnoticed. God hears your praise and will reward you for it.

David increased in his finances, relationships, and, most important of all, he praised his way right into heaven. Let's learn from David and have our praise become endless. A personal relationship with Jesus can help you. If you have not accepted Him, do it today and start your journey of endless praise. Your Heavenly Father awaits you.

God bless you!

Spiritual Afterburner

One of my fondest memories during my time in the United States Navy is an F-18 flyby. It was a clear afternoon, and the aircraft approached and hovered between two ships about twenty feet above the water. The pilot then "dropped the hammer," and we heard a loud *boom!* The afterburners were engaged, and fire was coming out from them.

We have a Father in Heaven with "beforeburners" and afterburners. Psalm 97:1–3 (NLT) says, "The Lord is king! Let the earth rejoice! Let the farthest coastlands be glad. Dark clouds surround him. Righteousness and justice are the foundation of his throne. Fire spreads ahead of him and burns up all his foes." Children of God have this assurance. He will fight our battles for us, so even while we are going through something, He is taking us through it. Anyone who is an enemy to a child of God automatically becomes an enemy of God. If our enemies aren't careful, the afterburners might consume them. Pray hard for your enemies to confess their sin and get saved. Some, because of their rebellion to living righteous, are experiencing the "beforeburners" and ultimately the afterburners will get them in the end. Don't delay. Get out of harm's way today and become a friend of God, not an enemy.

God bless you!

Rescue Me Quickly

When our backs are against the wall and our attackers are advancing, we need quick rescuing. This feeling of desperation may be caused by a lack of finances, health issues, relationship issues, and so on. In order to be safe as well as receive your divine protection, you need to call on the right God.

Let's take a look at what David prayed in Psalm 31:1–2 (NLT): "O Lord, I have come to you for protection; don't let me be disgraced. Save me, for you do what is right. Turn your ear to listen to me; rescue me quickly. Be my rock of protection, a fortress where I will be safe." David was rescued because he called upon the right God.

I don't know where you are today, but if you aren't praying to God the Father through His Son, Jesus Christ, you are missing out on life. Jesus will come to your rescue when you least expect it. Start trusting Him today. Step out in faith and believe that He will turn things around for your good. Be encouraged. He has not left you or forsaken you. Pray the prayer that King David prayed and ask, "Rescue me quickly, Father," and God will hear you and help you. Call on Him today.

God bless you!

Whom Do You Agree with?

Have you ever been asked to judge between friends? You're suddenly in an awkward position, not wanting to hurt the feelings of either one. Sometimes we choose to remain neutral and not agree with either party.

Many people believe they can remain neutral spiritually. Unfortunately, this is not possible. If we don't agree with Jesus, we automatically agree with Satan. Whomever we agree with determines whom we will walk with. This is what the Bible says in Amos 3:3 (NLT): "Can two people walk together without agreeing on the direction?"

The world knows the way they should live but still chooses not to agree to the terms of the contract. Followers of Jesus Christ, on the other hand, have agreed to the terms of the contract. Analyze yourself. Whom do you agree with by the way you live? Don't be fooled. The world also comes to church and shouts, "Praise the Lord! Hallelujah!" but then continues to live out their sin. They agree with Satan. True followers who agree with Jesus refrain from sin, even when it involves suffering. Again, my friends, I ask: whom do you agree with? Let it be Jesus.

God bless you!

Seeking the Lord's Help in Sickness

No one in their right mind looks forward to being sick. However, sickness finds our address from time to time. There are temporary illnesses, and sometimes severe illnesses, that people deal with on a daily basis. Let's talk a little on how to deal with it. The Bible gives us countless examples of people seeking and receiving the Lord's help for healing.

In the following area of scripture, we are going to look at King Asa, who did *not* seek God's help. The Bible says in 2 Chronicles 16:12–13(NLT): "In the thirty-ninth year of his reign, Asa developed a serious foot disease. Yet even with the severity of his disease, he did not seek the Lord's help but turned only to his physicians. So he died in the forty-first year of his reign." Please be advised that Asa was a man of God and pleasing to Him for many years. He was told by the prophet Azariah that whenever he sought God, he would find Him (2 Chronicles 15:2).

We have the same promise today, my friends. Don't allow your sickness to drown out your ability to seek the Lord and not just your physician. We serve a jealous God who looks forward to our dependence on Him for our healing. First, get your soul healed and sealed for heaven, and then physical healing will follow. Seek the Lord's help. He is willing and able. Pray without ceasing.

God bless you!

Guarantee for the Godly

I've heard it said, "Nothing in life is a guarantee." I disagree with that statement, and I'll tell you why. God gives us—His godly ones—many guarantees in this life and then in the life to come. Listen to this powerful guarantee in Psalm 97:10: "You who love the Lord, hate evil! He protects the lives of His godly people and rescues them from the power of the wicked."

That's powerful! However, we have a slight problem—or a big problem—and it's that people who claim to be godly are not letting go of evil in their lives. Instead of hating evil, they embrace evil. These actions break our agreement with God, and the guarantee no longer stands.

If you feel the powers of evil are prevailing over you, causing you to do and say things of an ungodly nature, it's time to put an end to it. Confess your sins today and get back on track. Establish—or reestablish—a love relationship with Jesus Christ, our Lord, in order to partake of all God's guarantees. Embrace a godly lifestyle, and God, who sees everything we do, will rescue you.

God bless you!

Crush Him

Christians often declare, "The enemy, Satan, is under my feet!" That declaration would be fine if it were truly put into action. Some so-called Christians have a serious disease called undercover sin. Sad to say, before Christ some Christians were less hypocritical. Let's change the "all talk and no walk" frame of mind and really crush Satan under our feet. The Apostle Paul explained how to successfully accomplish this in Romans 16:19–20: "I want you to be wise in doing right and to stay innocent of any wrong. The God of peace will soon crush Satan under your feet."

We must first seek the wisdom that God offers and abstain from sin. If our lives mirror this, we are truly crushing Satan under our feet. Don't stop crushing him until an angel locks him away for a thousand years. Be victorious over sin. Forgive all that sin against you. Love your enemies. In doing so, demons will be made miserable, but angels will rejoice. Don't lift your foot to see how Satan is doing down there. You cannot kill him, but you can surely defeat him by the power of the Holy Spirit.

What will you do today? Crush him or entertain him? Be wise and do what's right.

God bless you!

God Sees Your Troubles

The conversation started with a brokenhearted man telling his pastor that God does not see his troubles or He would have helped by now for sure. The pastor encouraged the brother in the Lord with this powerful area of scripture: Isaiah 40:27–29: "O Jacob, how can you say the Lord does not see your troubles? O Israel, how can you say God ignores your rights? Have you never heard? Have you never understood? The Lord is the everlasting God, the Creator of all the earth. He never grows weak or weary. No one can measure the depths of His understanding. He gives power to the weak and strength to the powerless."

My friends, if you are a born-again believer in Christ Jesus, you are the children of Israel. You are entitled to certain rights as royalty. Jesus promised tribulation, yes, but He didn't say every day will be a day of tribulation. Keep in mind: God did not forget you. He is working things out for you right now. Doors are being opened to bless you right now. Keep the faith. Your troubles will soon be gone in Jesus's name. Those without a personal relationship with Jesus Christ, you need to first open your heart and invite Him in, and then the same promises in His written Word will also apply to you. We must do our part by faith, and God will do His part and bless us.

God bless you!

Partial Heart

"I promise to love you with part of my heart for the rest of my life if you would take me as your husband (or wife)."

Although true in many marriages, that proposal would not be comforting to the potential bride or groom. The same is true spiritually. The bride of Christ—the church—often accepts Him with excitement, but deep in our hearts, we have a few conditions. Many have strayed from the faith because God did not grant what they expected when they expected it. This is how King David encouraged his son, Solomon, in 1 Chronicles 28:9: "And Solomon, my son, learn to know the God of your ancestors intimately. Worship and serve Him with your whole heart and a willing mind. For the Lord sees every heart and knows every plan and thought. If you seek Him you will find Him. But if you forsake Him, He will reject you forever."

My friends, it is so important to love the Lord with your whole heart, mind, and strength. Anything less will lead to spiritual bankruptcy. Many have gone that path not realizing that a partial love for God has made God reject them. They continue to go to church on Sunday and shout, "Hallelujah!" My advice to anyone in that state is to repent and repent fast. Get back on track. If you are not saved, get saved so you can have the eternal hope of heaven through Christ Jesus. God gave you your heart not to depart from Him but to give back to Him.

God bless you!

Be a Good Leader

Every one of us in some form or another has been appointed to lead. Some do a good job, while others really mess things up. It is necessary to be a good spiritual leader in order to get God's approval. Leadership stems from the pastor down to the newborn believer. The newborn believer can lead the unsaved to Christ with just a testimony. However, there are consequences for poor leadership.

Micah 3:1, 2, 4 says, 'I said, "Listen, you leaders of Israel! You are supposed to know right from wrong, but you are the very ones who hate good and love evil…Then you beg the Lord for help in times of trouble! Do you really expect Him to answer? After all the evil you have done, He won't even look at you!" Those are severe words toward poor leaders. My advice is simply this: repent of all evil. Turn to God with a willing heart to obey His Word and lead with authority. Whether you're a mom, a dad, a new believer, or a pastor, when the enemy sends demons to throw you offtrack, resist. Follow the leading of the Holy Spirit and go another way. When we exemplify good spiritual leadership, all other areas will be a breeze, and God will be pleased.

God bless you!

Spiritually Divide Your Eggs

Don't put all your eggs in one basket, they say. It would be tragic if the basket were to fall and all your eggs get broken. Another reason is you may not have access to your egg nest in one location, so multiple investments are better. The Bible says this in Ecclesiastes 11:1–2: "Send your grain across the seas, and in time, profits will flow back to you. But divide your investments among many places, for you do not know what risks might lie ahead."

First and foremost, the spirit of God wants us to invest in people. Share the love of God with everyone you meet. The returns on those investments are astronomical. God is not against wise investments to generate a better life for yourself and for your family. Just keep it holy. Investing in anything ungodly, perverse, or crooked will not be blessed by God; it will be cursed. If you follow the simple instructions of investing in human souls first, your spiritual discernment will increase causing you to make better personal investments.

Spiritually divide your eggs. Invest in God's business, and He will invest in yours.

God bless you!

Blessing and Cursing

Some really nice people have a bad habit of cursing. It becomes second, or even first, nature to them. Whether or not they have been aggravated by someone, the bad language pours out in abundance. This is a minor use of the word *curse* compared to when God is doing the cursing. God does not use indecent words; what He does is withdraw His blessings from the home or the wicked and apply a curse. Proverbs 3:33 says, "The Lord curses the house of the wicked, but He blesses the home of the upright."

Inquiring minds may wonder, who is "the wicked"? Anyone who knows what is wrong but willfully does it is wicked. You are wicked if you go to church every week and say you love God but refuse to forgive your neighbor. The upright, on the other hand, make every effort to live for God, serve Him daily, and obey His commands. The sins they commit are not premeditated. They exercise humility and embrace instruction.

Analyze yourself on a daily basis. Place yourself in line for the blessing, and I will do the same. Stop the curse now. Let's be all that God created us to be in Jesus's name.

God bless you!

Receiving Instructions

"Thou shalt not use the Lord's name in vain." Oh, that instruction is old. It doesn't apply anymore, does it? Yes, it does, and how sad that even Christians ignore this instruction.

Sometimes when we pray, we call the Lord's name repeatedly in vain. Remember the example prayer that Jesus gave. He said, "Hallowed be your name." He was instructing us to hallow the name of the Father or, in other words, give His name high reverence and respectful honor. Instructions for life are given throughout the Bible. The question is, how well do you receive them? Proverbs 10:8 says: "The wise are glad to be instructed, but babbling fools fall flat on their faces."

Don't frown upon the instructions in the Bible. Accept them and experience a life-changing relationship with Jesus Christ. It doesn't matter where you have been or what you have done, God can and will forgive you. The ball is in your court. Repent of your sins and start living. Receive instructions with joy and share the love of Jesus Christ in your world. Though at times the conviction does not feel good, all the instructions in the Bible are good.

God bless you!

Where Should I Take My Troubles?

I used to have so many troubles that it almost seemed like I was a hundred different people living in one body. What a catastrophe that was! To God be the glory, I no longer feel that way. When the weight of the world is on your shoulders, you have a hope in Jesus Christ. Take your troubles to Him. This is what the Bible says in Psalm 55:1–2: "Listen to my prayer, O God. Do not ignore my cry for help! Please listen and answer me, for I am overwhelmed by my troubles."

The Lord rescued David and brought peace in his life. He will do the same for you. Taking your troubles to people in the world who cannot help is a waste of time. Take your troubles to God through His Son, Jesus Christ, and watch Him send healing, peace, joy, and all things wonderful to you. Resist the devil. Cry out to your creator if you desire the best future on earth and unto forever.

God bless you!

Truth Machine

If you've ever taken a lie detector test, then you know that a series of questions, that will detect your body's response to telling the truth, are asked. When you lie, something changes in your heart. It beats a little faster, and, in some cases, your conscience may bug you. Many nonbelievers and believers in Jesus Christ have grown immune to lying. The person they lie to the most is themselves. They may say things like "My walk with God is just fine," when in truth it is not, or "I have a great marriage," when they actually don't. To correct this, we need to pattern what David says in Psalm 119:29: "Keep me from lying to myself; give me the privilege of knowing your instructions."

The ninth commandment says, don't bear false witness. In other words, don't lie. It's time to become a truth machine. Speak the truth. Speak it in love. Start by telling yourself the truth. Admit to yourself that you have a problem with anger, unforgiveness, or pornography, and then seek God's help. When you lay your problems down at the feet of Jesus, He will fix them. It starts when you choose to be truthful. When you are true to yourself, the truth will go forth to everyone else. The rewards for telling the truth are endless. God detests a lying tongue, but He embraces a person who speaks the truth.

God bless you!

I Need a Blessing Right Now

I need a blessing right now! My health is bad, my bills are due, my spouse is angry with me, and my dog ran away. There are many reasons why we may need a blessing right now. We are doing well, however, if we've already received the eternal blessings from God—for instance, salvation and a legacy of good will toward men. Those blessings reward us into eternity.

Your blessing need not only be monetary. There are many ways in which God blesses His people. In Genesis 32:26, Jacob wrestled with the angel of God for his blessing: "Then the man said, 'Let me go, for the dawn is breaking!' But Jacob said, 'I will not let you go unless you bless me.'" The angel of the Lord had to touch Jacob's hip and put it out of joint in order to break free. Jacob received his blessing, his name was changed to Israel, and his twelve sons became the twelve tribes of Israel. The rest is history. Talk about a legacy.

We too need to hold onto God and not let go until He blesses us. However, after receiving your blessing, don't let go, stay close to Him, and grow and grow. I need a blessing right now. I know your pain, and the giver of all good gifts will bless you in His special way. Just remember to seek the giver, not the gifts.

God bless you!

We Are Living When
We Are Praising Him

Most people in the world today are existing but not living. If you are a bit confused by that statement, please remember what Jesus told us—that He is the way, the truth, and the life. This simply means that real life, which is the spiritual life, can only be obtained through Him. To prove to ourselves and God that we belong to Him, our lives must reflect the ways of Christ. Our Lord Jesus praised the Father every day, letting the Pharisees and everyone know He is doing the will of the Father.

Let's start living by praising the Father. The Bible says this in Psalm 115:17–18: "The dead cannot sing praises to the Lord, for they have gone into the silence of the grave. But we can praise the Lord both now and forever!"

Praise the Lord. David loved to praise the Lord, so he obtained life eternally. Anyone planning to get to heaven should get accustomed to praising the Lord now because that is what we will be doing in heaven. Don't be alive in the church on Sundays and dead the rest of the week. Let your praises ring out. Greet people by saying, "Praise the Lord!" Sing songs of praise. Listen to praise music. Live in your praise, my friend, and only then will you be truly living.

God bless you!

Self-Harm

Imagine taking a knife, going to your bathroom, sitting in the tub, cutting both wrists, and then allowing yourself to bleed to death slowly. Most wouldn't ever consider doing that; however, there are some who do every year.

So what's the analogy, you might ask. It's simply this: we, as believers, tend to harm ourselves as well. Although not to the extreme of cutting our wrists, the Bible does say this in Proverbs 15:32: "If you reject discipline, you only harm yourself; but if you listen to correction, you grow in understanding." People who've cut their wrists didn't get to that point instantly; there were other factors that caused such a drastic decision. Similarly, Christians who allow different factors to take them off their right spiritual walk have cut their wrists spiritually and are slowly dying.

It's time to stop harming yourself and start helping yourself. Confess to Jesus Christ whether for the first time or a rededication. Stop bleeding away the Holy Spirit; retain Him. He wants to hang out with you. Listen to correction and grow in understanding. Put an end to self-harm. Both you and God will be glad you did.

God bless you!

Faith, Faith, Faith

You gotta have faith, faith, faith! This may bring to memory a famous pop song. However, the song was not talking about faith in God through Jesus Christ. As believers, we are to be rooted in our faith knowing that God will show up, not just believing that He can show up. The sad thing is many Christians have less than mustard seed faith in God. Here is my reason for saying this. Listen to Jesus's response to His disciples not being able to heal a boy with seizures. Matthew 17:20–21 says: "'You don't have enough faith,' Jesus told them. 'I tell you the truth, if you had faith even as small as a mustard seed, you could say to this mountain, "Move from here to there," and it would move. Nothing would be impossible.'"

Miracles can happen with mustard seed faith. A mustard seed is barely visible by the naked eye—that's how small it is. Let's work on getting some today. Faith comes by hearing the Word of God in or outside church by reading the Bible, through Bible studies, listening to Christian music, and the like. Start building your faith so you can be victorious over your mountains. Don't be like many who are full of doubt and remain in the stables. Through Jesus Christ, our Lord, open up those gates and start running the race to glory by faith.

God bless you!

Cheer Up

Whenever we feel down, we tend to look for someone or something to cheer us up. However, that cheer may only last a short time. There will come a day when the redeemed of the Lord will be cheerful in the presence of the Most High God. The prophet, Zephaniah, spoke about this in Zephaniah 3:16–17: "On that day the announcement to Jerusalem will be, 'Cheer up, Zion! Don't be afraid! For the Lord your God is living among you. He is a mighty savior. He will take delight in you with gladness. With His love, He will calm all your fears. He will rejoice over you with joyful songs.'"

I was blessed by this area of scripture. God is singing due to the actions of true Christians. If you do not compromise your walk with the Lord but you feel down, cheer up! God is with you and will reward you with a home in glory at just the right time. If you are working out a few things to get right, hurry! Don't miss the most important flight—the rapture. We, the people of God through Jesus Christ, will be under attack by the devil on a daily basis, but cheer up! My family, laugh at the devil. He wishes to be in our position, having reservations to heaven. Keep that smile.

God bless you!

Reverse Psychology

Many of us, Christian or not, use reverse psychology on our fellow men to prove a point or, perhaps, to show how smart we think we are. Some of us even try this foolishness with God. We justify our behaviors by partially lining them up with the Word of God. Pride and self-righteousness cause this.

Peter tried this in Matthew 18:21–22: "Then Peter came to him and asked, 'Lord, how often should I forgive someone who sins against me? Seven times?' 'No, not seven times,' Jesus replied, 'but seventy times seven!'" Peter's self-righteousness told him there was a cap on forgiveness, and he brought his theory to Jesus.

I am glad Peter used a bit of reverse psychology so we could learn about this thing called forgiveness. Who are we to not forgive and then justify it using scripture from the Bible? That, my friend, is using reverse psychology on yourself. Let's get it right by living a life that honors Jesus Christ. He forgave, and so should we. He loves, and so should we. Let's imitate Him.

God bless you!

Always Remember His Good Deeds

Ungrateful people are all around us, that is true. But what about us? Sometimes we are also ungrateful. We complain about what we don't have, worry about the future, and focus on our problems more than on our God. One effective method to maintain a healthy attitude of gratitude is to reflect on what God has done for you in the past. Sing praises to him for it. David says this in Psalm 9:11: "Sing praises to the Lord who reigns in Jerusalem. Tell the world about his unforgettable deeds."

We should never forget what God has done for us. Let's share our testimonies with believers and nonbelievers alike. Close the complaint department; it's not doing good business anyway. Instead, open a praise and thanksgiving department. Expand your ministry with the testimonies you have, proclaiming to the world all your Heavenly Father has blessed you with. Let's never forget where he has brought us from. It makes us more excited about where we are going.

God bless you!

Stop Complaining, Start Singing

"Lord, when will I get a break? I'm always broke, I can't pay my bills, my relationship is in shambles…" Many people are complaining these days. Sometimes we even complain to those who are in worse situations than we are.

Here's a challenge for you: each time you feel the urge to complain, sing a song instead. Don't know any modern worship songs? Sing "Jesus Loves the Little Children." Reflect on all the good that God has done for you. He woke you up this morning. He also gave you that mouth to sing praises to Him and not to complain to Him. David says this in Psalm 92:4: You thrill me, Lord, with all you have done for me. I sing for joy because of what you have done."

Singing songs of praise will cause God to open many doors of blessings to you. He looks forward to the praises of His people. Trust the Lord Jesus Christ with all your heart, cast your cares on Him, leave them there, and start singing.

God bless you!

Be Mindful of What You Listen to

If your ears are in good working condition, you will hear things. However, making the choice of what we listen to becomes more involved. We tend to listen to things of our own interest, which could be for our own benefit or for improving someone else's way of life. Those things are good, but what about the junk we listen to? What does it say about us?

Proverbs 17:4 says, "Wrongdoers eagerly listen to gossip; liars pay close attention to slander." A few powerful points: (1) If we eagerly look forward to juicy gossip, we are wrongdoers; (2) If we pay close attention to slander, we are liars. No wrongdoers or liars can enter the Kingdom of heaven. You might ask: why would listening to slander make me a liar? Well, think about it. Each time a story leaves from one person to another, it changes a little bit. So the very moment you open your mouth to pass on slander, you put someone down that may or may not be guilty of what is being said. To avoid the negative position of wrongdoing and lying, be mindful in your conversations. If a close friend or associate initiates such foolishness, ask them to stop or excuse yourself from the conversation. You cannot control what people say, but you can control what you listen attentively to. Listen to the Holy Spirit.

God bless you!

Forgiving Power

In today's society, there are many people who crave power—monetary power, leadership power, and even dictatorship power. Likewise, it is sad when we look around and realize that many are lacking two of the most important powers we should have: the power to love and the power to forgive. These are powers because without the power of the Holy Spirit himself helping us, we are unable to love or forgive to the full extent in which those words mean.

One of the most powerful stories about forgiveness is found in Acts 7:59–60. It says, "As they stoned him, Stephen prayed, 'Lord Jesus, receive my spirit.' He fell to his knees, shouting, 'Lord, don't charge them with this sin!' And with that he died." As they stoned Stephen, he forgave them. Now that's power from on high. The natural man would want to grab a stone and retaliate. However, the spiritual man endowed with power from Jesus is able to forgive. We must love our enemies, and then forgiving them will come supernaturally. Trying to forgive without love is impossible. True forgiveness results from true love. Acquire the power today. His name is Jesus. Accept Him, and then you can live, love, and forgive.

God bless you!

The Range of God's Love

I've come across many individuals who tell me God does not love them. "If He loved me, why would this happen to me?" Our circumstances do not determine God's love for us. The mere fact that we were even born proves His love for us, and, on top of it, He sent His only begotten Son, Jesus, to die on the cross for us. God's love goes far and wide, high in the sky and deep below. David says this in Psalm 36:5: "Your unfailing love, O Lord, is as vast as the Heavens; your faithfulness reaches beyond the clouds."

Whether in a submarine or a space shuttle, we will never be out of range for God's love. Never forget that. Rather than question His love for you, you ought to question your love for Him. Jesus said, "If you loved me, you would obey my commands." God loves us beyond measure. Even He must keep His commands. Without the shedding of blood, there is no forgiveness of sin. That is why Jesus came, lived a sin-free life, and died on the cross so we could be forgiven through His righteousness. Now that is love to the highest degree. How well do you reciprocate?

God bless you!

Take Care of My Sheep

We all have things that need to be taken care of. Bills, relationships, work, among others. On top of these, believers have a very special task, which is to take care of God's sheep. It is one of the ways in which we prove to Jesus that we really do love Him.

John 21:16 (NLT) tells of a conversation between Jesus and Peter: "Jesus repeated the question: 'Simon son of John, do you love me?' 'Yes Lord,' Peter said, 'you know I love you.' 'Then take care of my sheep,' Jesus said."

Peter denied Christ three times, and now he's commissioned by Jesus to represent Him. Maybe you have failed Jesus in the past, but today is your day to shake the dust off and shine for the King.

Tell everyone that Jesus is Lord of your life and that He's coming back soon. Don't be ashamed of the Gospel; instead, proclaim the Gospel, and that, my friends, will be taking care of His sheep.

God bless you!

Don't Play the Blame Game

Doesn't it make you angry when you're blamed for something you didn't do? Even if you did it and you're blamed for it, you still get a little upset. Therefore, we should keep this in mind with regard to others who, like us, have feelings too.

Wrongful blame may be out of our control in most cases, but the way to avoid justifiable blame is to do what is right. Now there is another blame a bit more severe. It's when we blame someone other than ourselves to escape punishment from God. Listen to what Adam said to God when he was busted for sinning in Genesis 3:12: "The man replied, 'It was the woman you gave me who gave me the fruit, and I ate it.'" Rather than saying, "Forgive me, Lord, I messed up," Adam shifted the blame to his wife.

Let's not blame others for our bad choices, sexual sin, ungodly outbursts, not getting ahead, poor or no spiritual growth…and the list goes on—you fill in the blanks. Let's take responsibility for our own actions, confess our sins to God, and watch him do miracles in our lives. Don't play the blame game, or Jesus will look upon you with shame.

God bless you!

Very Clear and Present Danger

When driving along the roadways, we see danger signs warning us of sharp turns, slippery roads, or steep cliffs. The highway safety board does its best to make these danger signs very clear.

Human beings have something or someone who is a very clear and present danger. That danger is never absent from our lives in the spiritual realm because the devil wants to kill us (John 10:10). That is one form of danger to pray about. Then, there is physical danger to pray about as David did in Psalm 7:1–2: "I come to you for protection, O Lord my God. Save me from my persecutors—rescue me! If you don't, they will maul me like a lion, tearing me to pieces with no one to rescue me."

We won't see all danger from Satan that surrounds us because he is slick. Be sure to keep the whole armor of God on at all times. Never fear those presenting danger to you. Drive fear in them by revealing God in you. If God is not leading your life, start today by accepting Jesus Christ as Lord and Savior. Jesus never said there wouldn't be danger, but He did say He'd always be with you. Call on Him and face your very clear and present danger with a victorious mindset.

God bless you!

Take the Way Out

The murder suspect on trial confesses to the jury, "I didn't mean to shoot him. The devil made me do it." The devil gets blamed for many things that we choose to do. Yes, our enemy Satan presents the temptation, but we are the ones who choose to indulge rather than take the way out. You may be thinking, what way out? Well, this is what the Bible says in 1 Corinthians 10:13: "The temptations in your life are no different from what others experience. And God is faithful. He will not allow the temptation to be more than you can stand. When you are tempted, He will show you a way out so that you can endure."

Wow! I didn't know the Bible says that. My friend, it is so important to read the Bible. Our spiritual eyes are opened when we accept Jesus Christ as Lord and Savior. We begin to understand what the Bible is saying when we read it. The way out of temptation becomes clearer and easier to take when the Holy Spirit reveals it to us. On the other hand, when we are surrounded by darkness and our spiritual eyes are blindfolded, we can forget it. It's a losing battle.

Get connected to the Holy Spirit. Be victorious. Satan will tempt you, but God will show you the way out. Take the way out.

God bless you!

When You Feel Helpless

It is a bad feeling to be helpless in any situation. The bills are due, and you don't have a clue. Your health is failing, and your mind is ailing. Well, you get the picture. Sometimes those feelings may arise, but our victorious outcome is based on who we know. Those who know the Lord, the source of our help, can cry out to Him anytime without making a reservation.

The Bible says in Psalm 10:17, "Lord, you know the hopes of the helpless. Surely you will hear their cries and comfort them."

Cry out to the Lord when you feel helpless and watch Him work. His word is true. Heaven and earth will fade away, but His word will never fail. We often make the mistake of trying to fix a really bad situation on our own only to fail miserably. Don't stress yourself or add to your depression, my friend. Turn to God. If you already know Him, cry out to Him. There is no need to reinvent the spiritual wheel that's turning. Get busy about God's business and watch Him turn a hopeless situation into a blessed one. Cry out to Him and, most importantly, live for Him.

God bless you!

Don't Run to the Hills

Calamity strikes. You are looking for a way out, so you run to the hills. Maybe you already live in Beverly Hills or Hollywood Hills, so you flee to a mountain to hide. Let me lovingly say this: seeking help from the wrong source will add to your negative situation. A hill or mountain cannot help you. People who mean well but are not connected to God will never administer the proper spiritual comfort. Listen to what the Bible says in Psalm 121:1–2: "I look up to the mountains—does my help come from there? My help comes from the Lord, who made Heaven and Earth!" The Spirit of God is saying that He is our help. Instead of running away from Him, run to Him. I once saw a woman in a mall's food court crying uncontrollably. I introduced myself as a pastor and asked if there was anything she wanted me to keep in prayer. She responded, "No thanks."

It's sad how many people depend on everyone and everything else but God to get them through. If you're thinking you don't believe in God, well guess what? He believes in you. That is why you are alive today. He has work for you to do. This life is not about us; it's about Him. Don't run to the hills; run to Jesus, the King.

God bless you!

Spare the Ear

I recently witnessed a bad car accident. It started with Motorist A in an SUV trying to get by Motorist B. Motorist B purposely slammed on his brakes causing Motorist A to also slam on his brake, screeching his tires. This led to an all-out road rage with both vehicles traveling at high speeds. Motorist A swung to avoid hitting Motorist B, lost control of the SUV, which jumped the median, and collided head on with another SUV.

I said a quick prayer for the lives of everyone involved. Motorist A had three young boys in the backseat whom he was taking to school and another adult in the front passenger side. Everyone was alive, thank God. This jaw-dropping experience reminds me of the apostle Peter jumping into war mode and forgetting the law of love. Luke 22:50–51 says this: "And one of them struck at the high priest's slave, slashing off his right ear. But Jesus said, 'No more of this.' And he touched the man's ear and healed him."

Spare the ear, my friends. Don't allow your temper to get the best of you. Pray before you act or react. Live a life that gives God the glory in Jesus's name. Love will always triumph over anger.

God bless you!

Selective Comfort

We all seek comfort in one way or another. For some, it's a nice home, vehicle, and finances. For others, it's comforting to know their relationship with God is in right standing. Whatever you find comfort in is what you make a priority in your life. Let me encourage you to involve Jesus on your list of priorities. He will give you a comfort like never before. The Bible says this in 2 Corinthians 1:3–4: "All praise to God, the Father of our Lord Jesus Christ. God is our merciful Father and the source of all comfort. He comforts us in all our troubles so that we can comfort others. When they are troubled, we will be able to give them the same comfort God has given us."

Many feel God had nothing to do with their wealth, success, and financially comfortable lifestyle. They are wrong. God is the source of all comfort. However, there is more to it than that. Many people are comfortable in the world but uncomfortable in the spiritual realm of things. It is more important to be comfortable with God. Money and status do not guarantee peace and joy. Only a right relationship with Jesus Christ can. Am I saying we won't have trials? Absolutely not, but through our trials, He will comfort us. Be sure your selective comfort honors God. Make Him priority, and you'll be glad you did.

God bless you!

Wisdom versus Evil

I find it sad to hear evil people brag about how wise they are. First of all, wisdom comes from God. People may be knowledgeable in some things, but there is no genuine wisdom without the Holy Spirit. Are you being led by the Holy Spirit, proving you are wise? It all depends on your discernment, good judgment, and overall fear of the Lord. Proverbs 8:12–13 (NLT) says this: "I, Wisdom, live together with good judgment. I know where to discover knowledge and discernment. All who fear the Lord will hate evil. Therefore, I hate pride and arrogance, corruption and perverse speech." So, we who are wise should hate evil and all its attributes. Those are rage, pride, arrogance, lust, sexual immorality, lying, and unforgiveness, which tie into murder in the heart toward another human being.

Stay away from all evil. If you choose to cling to evil, then you are not wise. You are fooling yourself by ruling yourself. You may believe luck is on your side, and you are absolutely right because luck is of the devil. When you acquire wisdom, you are blessed by God. Then, you truly have the victory. Choose today whom you will serve—the Lord Jesus Christ or yourself? Choose wisely.

God bless you!

Save Yourselves

Have you ever asked someone, "Are you saved?" and they answer in a roundabout way? They say, "My father is a pastor," or "My mother goes to church every Sunday." They fail to give a straight answer, don't they? Chances are, those who respond in that manner are lacking their own personal relationship with Jesus.

The Bible says this in Ezekiel 14:13–14 (NLT): "Son of Man, suppose the people of a country were to sin against me, and I lifted my fist to crush them, cutting off their food supply and sending a famine to destroy both people and animals. Even if Noah, Daniel, and Job were there, their righteousness would save no one but themselves, says the Sovereign Lord."

If these well-known men of God could not save the ungodly, then Mom or Pop cannot save you either. We must save ourselves by establishing our own personal relationship with Jesus. Then, be bold with your faith. Shine your light so others can follow your example. In Matthew 7:23, Jesus says to the unsaved, "I never knew you. Get away from me." Don't allow this world to drag you away from Jesus. Run to Him and save yourself.

God bless you!

Why Be on Your Own

People love to say they are independent. Some have the "I don't need anyone" attitude. While that may be fine to a certain degree, it's a problem when it pertains to God. The Bible tells us that there are godly people and wicked people. It sounds harsh, but what makes a person wicked is not what they do but what they fail to do. The sin of omission covers a wide range of sin, including failure to accept Jesus Christ as Lord and Savior and to live for Him. Many people do great things for man but choose to ignore great things they could be doing for God.

Never forget what God says in Psalm 1:6 (NLT): "For the Lord watches over the path of the godly, but the path of the wicked leads to destruction." Don't remain on your own without the King of Kings. Accept Him today while there is still time. Look at all the natural disasters happening around us. Pay attention to the signs—they are everywhere to see. God often gives warning before striking, which is why He sent so many prophets and then ultimately His son. The wise person will listen, stop trying to do it on their own, turn to Jesus Christ, and accept free salvation needed for their heavenly home.

God bless you!

Forever Working Word

The Word of God is truly alive and working in the hearts of mankind. Anyone who hears the Word of God is touched by it in some form or another, so we should always be ready to speak it. Anyone who speaks the Word of God is actually representing God to the person they are speaking to. You who speak the Word of God to encourage, educate, elevate, and correct may be the only Jesus that person will ever see.

When we are received by listening ears, rejoice. Be glad and pray for the people you encounter that the Word keeps on working. The Bible says this in 1 Thessalonians 2:13: "Therefore, we never stop thanking God that when you received His message from us, you didn't think of our words as mere human ideas. You accepted what we said as the very word of God—which, of course, it is. And this word continues to work in you who believe."

Continue reading God's Word with great excitement and allow the Holy Spirit Himself to use you. Believers have a great opportunity to plant seeds of the Word of God into everyone we come in contact with, saved or unsaved. Living the Word and not only speaking it is proof that God's Word is working in you.

God bless you!

Financing Available

Many people struggle to obtain financing when making a major purchase—for instance, a house, a car, or a commercial property. What an awesome feeling when the bank or lending institution grants approval! What an even better feeling if the funds are donated without having to repay!

Here's food for the thought: every human being alive is right now being financed by God. The great thing is we don't have to repay Him for the air we breathe. It would be quite a different story if we all had to carry oxygen tanks on our backs. Whether we choose to acknowledge this fact or not, God finances our lives. He also wants to finance our God-given aspirations and dreams. We first need to make sure our worship is real and that we are not trying to use God as a genie.

He says this in Psalm 50:10: "For all the animals of the forest are mine, and I own the cattle on a thousand hills." God grew weary of people attending the temple gathering making sacrifices with unclean hearts. He reminds us that He owns everything, and He desires to bless His people with His resources. Allow God to first finance your eternal salvation, and then all other desires you have will come to pass. Apply today.

God bless you!

A Trap Frequently Overlooked

"I am a Christian," says the twenty-one-year-old college woman to a man she is interested in having a future with. The man responds, "I know. I am a Christian too, but we have been dating for six months, and I feel it's time to take our relationship to another level."

The woman submitted to his request and participated in activity God created for the marriage bed. She felt disappointment and shame at first, but she grew more comfortable with her sin as time passed on. The man died in a tragic accident one month later. Some may say it is a "cow-incidence" but personally I've never seen two cows crash. The Bible says this in Proverbs 28:10: "Those who lead the upright into sin will fall into their own trap, but the honest will inherit good things."

Many have caused God's people to stray. Be careful. Don't lie, cheat, or cause harm to God's people causing them to say or do something sinful. You will pay for it. We are God's sheep. He is the shepherd, and His duty is to protect the flock. God will punish "wolves" by allowing them to fall into the trap set for us. Saved or unsaved, think twice before causing God's son or daughter to sin. Don't fall into the trap frequently overlooked.

God bless you!

Corner Office

Dave, a prominent attorney earning a six-figure salary, became bitter after his boss informed him that a corner office would not be available to him. Dave had worked hard for seven years and often dreamed of having a corner office. After all, only the better attorneys got the corner office. Well, Dave quit the firm and got a job earning thirty thousand dollars per year less in order to have a corner office. We may look at this scenario and say, "He must be crazy!" but many people consider status of great importance. They must have the best home, the best car, the best jewelry, the best wife, the best husband, the best dog…you get the picture.

Interestingly, listen to what Jesus says in Luke 14:8–10: "When you are invited to a wedding feast, don't sit in the seat of honor. What if someone who is more distinguished than you has also been invited? The host will come and say, 'Give this person your seat.' Then you will be embarrassed…Instead, take the lowest place…Then when your host sees you, he will come and say, 'Friend, we have a better place for you!' For those who exalt themselves will be humbled, and those who humble themselves will be exalted."

The best status to have in this life is to know Jesus personally as Lord and Savior and to live for Him each day. Don't pray only when you need something but pray without ceasing each day. Call on Him today and watch Him exalt you.

God bless you!

Reaching for Jesus

To what degree do we reach for Jesus? Is it only when calamity strikes? Is it when we have nothing else to do? Or is it routine on a Sunday morning? If we truly understood the gift of salvation and the Lord Jesus Christ, we would reach for Him a lot more. Luke 19:1–4 tell us, "Jesus entered Jericho and made His way through the town. There was a man there named Zacchaeus. He was the chief tax collector in the region, and he had become very rich. He tried to get a look at Jesus, but he was too short to see over the crowd. So he ran ahead and climbed a sycamore-fig tree beside the road, for Jesus was going to pass that way."

You see, even though Zacchaeus was rich, he didn't have peace. He needed to reach out to the Prince of Peace. Zacchaeus didn't just look for Jesus with his eyes but with his heart. We need to do the same. Reach out to Jesus with our hearts daily. He is not passing by; Jesus is here, willing and able to receive our love offering. To prove our love for Jesus, our actions must align with our hearts. Zacchaeus climbed a tree, but we may have to climb a mountain. Let nothing or no one hinder you from reaching for Jesus. Fellowship, pray, read, and fast. Make the effort and reach for Him.

God bless you!

Eat the Bread of Life

Many people are bread lovers, and I am one of them. I love me some good, old-fashioned, Jamaican hard dough bread. It's also made in wheat. However, my favorite bread is not baked. He is the Bread of Life. If you are a little puzzled, let's check out a conversation Jesus had with some whom He just fed natural bread.

In John 6:33–35, Jesus says, "'The true bread of God is the one who comes down from heaven and gives life to the world.' 'Sir,' they said, 'give us that bread every day.' Jesus replied, 'I am the bread of life. Whoever comes to me will never be hungry again. Whoever believes in me will never be thirsty.'"

Knowing how much we love our bellies, we are no different from the five thousand-plus who followed Jesus for the food. Nothing against natural food like bread, just as long as spiritual bread is also being eaten. You will starve spiritually if you don't eat spiritual bread every day. Once a week is not good enough. Many Christians try once a week and die spiritually, lacking the Bread of Life. Involve daily devotional time in your routine. Read the Word. Pray without ceasing. Tell others about the Bread of Life and watch your own life skyrocket with joy and peace. Eat your fill today.

God bless you!

Grand Opening

Whenever a restaurant or store does a grand opening, they usually offer the public money saving deals in order to attract more customers. A local Chick-fil-A restaurant offered free chicken sandwiches. That sounded good to me, so after that, I was there on the regular. Those things are good, but there is another grand opening that I am waiting for. Revelation 21:1–2 says, "Then I saw a new Heaven and a new Earth, for the old Heaven and the old Earth had disappeared. And the sea was also gone. And I saw the holy city, the new Jerusalem, coming down from God out of Heaven like a bride beautifully dressed for her husband."

What a day that will be when we occupy the newly remodeled earth. The earth as we know it will be totally cleansed by fire. Then we will have a grand opening of the new earth, which will welcome the Holy City. This Holy City is the new Jerusalem created only for followers of Jesus Christ, not for mere believers in Jesus Christ. The reason is this: Satan believes in Jesus and fears Him; however, Satan does not do God's will. When we believe, we need to live for Him. In doing so, we remain holy. Why is it so important to remain holy? Simply this: only holy people can live in the Holy City. Check your status today and be ready for the Grand Opening.

God bless you!

Be Ready to Explain

Some people are shy. They don't initiate conversation or confront certain matters. It's to their disadvantage in many ways. The church, on the other hand, should pray for boldness. Although often ridiculed because of our faith, Christians must be bold enough to lovingly explain the Gospel.

The apostle Peter says in 1 Peter 3:15 (NLT): "If someone asks about your Christian hope, always be ready to explain it." Please keep in mind that as a believer you are not in the reserves for Christ's army; you are actively enlisted. Let's start proclaiming the Good News so the lost can be found. Many times the devil shut us up, and another soul remains lost because of our timid or "I can't be bothered" mentality.

It's time to shake off the old and bring in a new attitude, one that explains the Gospel of Jesus Christ with clarity. Jesus died on the cross for our sins, God raised Him from the dead on the third day, and He now lives forever. He offers the free gift of salvation to anyone who would believe and receive Him. Since we've received Him, God will raise us up on the last day too. Live with Jesus. Take it or leave it—that's the Gospel. Now tell it.

God bless you!

A Controlling Spirit

There are many forms of controlling spirits. Some are highly visible with spiritual eyes, while others are seasonal and discreet. Anger is a controlling spirit if you allow it. We are given opportunities to get angry on a daily basis, but to what degree are we allowing anger to take us? If we get really hot under the collar, then we are over one hundred degrees, and that's not cool at all.

The Bible says in Psalm 4:4: "Don't sin by letting anger control you. Think about it overnight and remain silent." Be sure to keep this in mind when driving on the roadways, arguing with spouse, friends, coworkers, or strangers. Controlling spirits attached to anger will have you in a world of hatred and vengeance.

You are much wiser than that, my friends. Fight the controlling evil spirit with the Holy Spirit. Forgive your offender immediately. Don't even waste time thinking of why you should hold them up in your heart. If Jesus can forgive us for all the wrongs we've done and not be angry with us for an extended period of time, we can do the same. Let's control our anger, or our anger will control us.

God bless you!

Some Dos and Don'ts When Fasting

Let me start by saying that fasting is a great way to get closer to God and place your body under the control of your spirit man. Some use fasting as a means of dieting. Although it works, fasting was not intended for that. Fasting is designed to enhance our spiritual being. When fasting, let's be sure our hearts are at peace with our fellow man. Don't be angry with someone or fast so that God can break their legs because someone's made you mad. That is not a fast that honors God. As a matter of fact, look at what God says in Isaiah 58:4: "What good is fasting when you keep on fighting and quarreling? This kind of fasting will never get you anywhere with me."

We should be loving, forgiving, patient, kind and other people centered at all times but especially when we are fasting! Abstaining from food is only the beginning of fasting. Sometimes, you have to leave the social arena when fasting if nothing Holy is being said. Feed the hungry, help the needy, and forgive your offender as Jesus did toward his persecutors while on the cross. Fast in this way and you will definitely get results from God. Cry out to Him in fasting and prayer, and He will see you through. Be quick to fast and slow to get angry.

God bless you!

Stop Stealing His Praise

Praise the Lord!

Very well said, indeed. We should never stop praising Him. When man attempts to praise us, we should always direct the praise to God. God looks forward to our praise. If we aren't praising Him, then we are robbing Him of His due praise. The Bible says this in Psalm 48:1 (NLT): "How great is the Lord, how deserving of praise, in the city of our God, which sits on His Holy mountain!"

God deserves our praise, even if we don't receive another blessing from Him. If we are breathing, we should be giving praise. Listen to music, which gives Him praise. Watch TV programming that gives Him praise. And get this: Allow your conversations to give Him praise!

Praising God is a lifestyle, not just a Sunday morning event. Our choice is simple: we either praise our Heavenly Father or keep the praise to ourselves, hence, robbing God. There are many great reasons to praise God, but the main reason we should praise Him is because of who He is—Lord God Almighty. Yes, Lord God Almighty. Let it sink in your spirit and then shout "Hallelujah!" which is the highest praise.

God bless you!

No Need to Know

Some people acquire the title Mr. or Mrs. Know-It-All due to the knowledge they have. There are some things we need to know and other things we shouldn't worry about. It is normal for us to want to know where we are going before leaving a starting point. There are many places we don't know, and there are many things we still don't know.

Let's face it: no one truly knows it all. In fact, only God knows it all. Here's an example of something we don't need to know. The Bible says in Acts 1:6–7: "So when the apostles were with Jesus, they kept asking Him, 'Lord, has the time come for you to free Israel and restore our kingdom?' He replied, 'The Father alone has the authority to set those dates and times, and they are not for you to know.'"

In a world where so many false prophets are predicting the end, we must be careful and not get caught up in their foolishness. Live each day being ready and then you won't have to worry over when your last day will be. Whether someone dies of natural causes or in a motor vehicle accident, that is the last day for that person. We can only hope the individual was ready to go. We don't need to know when the end will be, we only need to know that we are ready to go with God.

God bless you!

For or Against

Twelve jurors sit down to discuss a case. Six are in favor of the guilty verdict, while the other six are against it. Talk about a deliberation that will last a long time before everyone agrees. In a sense, we are all spiritual jurors who will give ourselves and those we influence a verdict of "guilty" or "not guilty." It really depends on whether or not we do the Lord's will. Attending church is a good start, but are we working with the Lord by doing His will?

Jesus says in Matthew 12:30 (NLT), "Anyone who isn't with me opposes me, and anyone who isn't working with me is actually working against me." In today's fast-paced world, it is easy to work against the Lord. Please keep in mind that we were created to work for the Lord, not against Him. Don't get it confused. God will meet our every need if we make the Kingdom of Heaven our primary concern.

What is number one on your agenda? Be honest with yourself. If it is not the will of God for mankind to become saved, it is time to change some things around. Start working with the Lord and you can expect great rewards both now and forever. Don't ignore the call and remain an enemy to our Lord because His enemies must fall. Begin working with Him today.

God bless you!

Build the Right Buildings

In the construction industry, contractors build buildings for their clients. They build everything from houses to skyscrapers. Globally, we have some spectacular-looking buildings. While this is all well and good, I can't help thinking about the conversation between Jesus and His disciples. Mark 13:1–2 says: "As Jesus was leaving the Temple that day, one of His disciples said, 'Teacher, look at these magnificent buildings! Look at the impressive stones in the walls.' Jesus replied, 'Yes, look at these great buildings. But they will be completely demolished. Not one stone will be left on top of another!'"

Here we can clearly see that we shouldn't spend all our energy building earthly buildings. We should build the right buildings in Heaven by sending up building blocks daily. Someone might ask, "What's involved with sending up building blocks?" Well, you start when you confess your sins to God and accept Jesus Christ into your heart as Lord and Savior. Next, you need to live for Him by following His lead. Contractors follow a blueprint to complete the project, and we must do the same. The Bible is our blueprint. Abide by it and be ready for heaven, which is our great completion, or ignore it and erect a faulty building that will crumble under pressure. Your building will last forever when you build on a firm foundation—Jesus Christ, the rock.

God bless you!

A Sweet Perfume

Upon meeting someone, one of two things may happen: their actions and/or conversation leave us with pleasant memories, or the experience leaves us with a bad taste in our mouth. So, what about ourselves? Do we leave a sweet fragrance at completion of conversation with friends or first-time conversants?

The Bible says this in 2 Corinthians 2:14: "But thank God! He has made us His captives and continues to lead us along in Christ's triumphal procession. Now He uses us to spread the knowledge of Christ everywhere, like a sweet perfume."

Perfume makers strive to produce captivating aromas that keep consumers wanting more. The same is true for the witness of Christ Jesus. He wants us to speak and live in such a way that others long to spend more time around us. If our conversations glorify God, it is well. If not, our so-called perfume will be a stench.

Don't leave a bad smell. Become a sweet-smelling perfume. You never know who you are witnessing to—perhaps, the next Sunday schoolteacher, deacon, or even a pastor. In these last days, we may not get a second chance to smell great, so make the most of the first opportunity.

God bless you!

Self-Protection

Protection is a major component in our society. We buy firearms and ferocious dogs and install burglar alarm systems to keep safe. Some study martial arts to defend themselves. However, if we truly consider things, all of our earthly defense systems can possibly fail. My advice for true protection is a right relationship with Jesus Christ. We are truly secure in Him.

The Bible tells us in Psalm 121:4–8, "Indeed, He who watches over Israel never slumbers or sleeps. The Lord Himself watches over you! The Lord stands beside you as your protective shade. The sun will not harm you by day, nor the moon at night. The Lord keeps you safe from all harm and watches over your life. The Lord keeps watch over you as you come and go, both now and forever."

So it is written, my friend, that we who live for God are well-protected. What about those who don't live for Him? It means they rely on self-protection, which has no guarantee.

Allow God to protect you. Accept His free gift of salvation and then stand secure and well-protected in Him.

God bless you!

Did You Find It?

It bugs me to look for something a long time and not find it, especially when I am sure of where I left it. When I do find it, what a relief! I say to my wife, Loretta, with excitement, "Guess what? I found what I was looking for!"

The Bible tells us to find something of great value as well and what will happen when we do find it. Luke 15:8–10 says this: "Or suppose a woman has ten silver coins and loses one. Wont she light a lamp and sweep the entire house and search carefully until she finds it? And when she finds it, she will call in her friends and neighbors and say,' Rejoice with me because I have found my lost coin.' In the same way, there is joy in the presence of God's angels when even one sinner repents."

Some people have been fortunate in their earthly findings of gold, oil, a compatible spouse, or a well-paying job. While those are all good if those same individuals die without finding salvation through Jesus Christ, they would have missed the most valuable of findings. So, in your search to discover why you are here on earth, accept Jesus into your life, and His Holy Spirit will give you the answers you need to know. Let me encourage you: find that relationship today and get to know Him better each day, and you will be glad you did.

God bless you!

Whose World Is It Anyway?

Growing up as children, we may have asked ourselves, "What would it be like to rule the world?" Well, it's really a tall order to fill, yet many have tried. It's amazing how so many people refuse to give God credit for being the creator and caretaker of this world. The Bible says this in Psalm 24:1: "The earth is the Lord's, and everything in it. The world and all its people belong to Him."

When we analyze our lives and look at the grand scheme of things, the intelligent person knows it points toward God. The not-so intelligent will listen to the Lord of this world. God has given him—Satan, that is—the authority to lead many down the unrighteous path. Satan is somewhat like a governor, but he is not the King who makes the final decision. Many are deceived in thinking partnership with evil will get them a great position in this world, and then they die and that's it.

What a lie that is! The truth is that there is another side to this life we now live. We set the stage for eternity with the King in Paradise or for eternity with the Governor in torment. Governors and presidents can be replaced, but kings have no time limit.

Who is your allegiance directed to? Choose wisely.

God bless you!

Give Him Thanks and Sing

Like many other people, I am a music lover. I love to sing songs of praise and listen to music giving God glory. Worship is one of many ways to give God thanks for all He has done, all He is doing, and all He will do. The Bible says this in Psalm 7:17: "I will thank the Lord because He is just; I will sing praises to the name of the Lord most high." God adores our praise, worship, and thanks. You can rest assured that our thankful hearts will be recognized by Him.

Some feel they are only qualified to sing in the shower, so they keep quiet in public. A way to look at it is like this: God kept you alive in the midst of your trials and sorrows, so you should sing to Him with the same voice He gave you to do so with. If everyone sounded the same, it would be boring to God, so He made us with our own unique voice.

So, how thankful are you to Him? Are you thankful enough to forget about man and sing your heart out to Him? Don't know any songs of praise? Learn some. God looks forward to the birds singing, so imagine how much more He looks forward to hearing from us. Don't just sing to Him on Sunday mornings in church. Sing to Him on a daily basis and watch Him reward you overwhelming peace and unspeakable joy. Give Him thanks and sing.

God bless you!

It's a Brand-New Day

When we think of all the potential a brand-new day has, we should get excited. If you are a child of God, you should have great expectations for each day. Even the unsaved have high expectations. How much more should we knowing that we have the favor of God?

Miracles happen every day, but keep in mind that we sometimes need to be the miracle as God works through us to bless someone else. So many people are sitting around waiting for their miracle. Please stop it. Go out and make things happen. It's a brand-new day! Don't spend it exactly like yesterday. The Bible tells a story about four men with leprosy who went out and received a miracle instead of sitting down doing nothing. It says in 2 Kings 7:8–9: "When the lepers arrived at the edge of the camp, they went into one tent after another, eating and drinking wine; and they carried off silver and gold and clothing and hid it. Finally they said to each other, this is not right. This is a day of Good News and we aren't sharing it with anyone."

Make your day more exciting. Share the Good News about Jesus Christ with someone. I guarantee you it will brighten your day. That person may receive the Lord or decide to come to church. You will be on cloud nine. Always remember this life is not about us. It's all about Jesus. Let each of your days reflect that.

God bless you!

A Season of Restoration

Anyone who's had plenty but is now experiencing lack is looking forward to a season of restoration. Time changes from one day to the next; no one knows what tomorrow may bring. If you have been robbed, mistreated, or abandoned, God is able to restore you. Your life is not over because a spouse walked out on you, or the boss fired you. The Lord will rescue you and restore you to your rightful place.

The Bible says this in Psalm 14:7: "Who will come from Mount Zion to rescue Israel? When the Lord restores His people, Jacob will shout with joy and Israel rejoice."

I truly believe that if you are the redeemed of the Lord or Israel, this is our season of restoration. Ultimately, God will restore us to our royalty state once we get to heaven and see Jesus face-to-face. However, we will be restored here on Earth as the Lord sees fit. Some of us may even exceed our original status. Promotion comes from the Lord, so when He restores you, stay humble and give Him praise. He gives and takes away—it is Him who is in charge. If you are not saved, become a part of Israel. Confess your sins to Jesus Christ so that your soul will be restored to your Maker. Salvation is the foundation to our restoration. It is your season.

God bless you!

Are You a Crowd Pleaser?

Most people want to be accepted by everyone. Many times we're pleasing to some, but others may not care for us. As the old saying goes: "Well, you can't please everybody." I have more to add to that: When you become a true follower of Jesus Christ, your crowd pleasing lessens more and more with each passing day. The reason is this: darkness is afraid of the Light in us believers, so they accept what is accursed just to hold on to their own philosophy.

This is what the Bible says in Galatians 1:9–10: "I say again what we have said before. If anyone preaches any other Good News than the one you welcomed, let that person be accursed. Obviously, I'm not trying to win the approval of people but of God. If pleasing people were my goal, I would not be Christ's Servant."

Trying to please the world, including those in church, will drain you. Focus on pleasing God because He cares for you. People often care for you when you have something to offer, but God cares for you just as you are. Remember: we will always be pleasing to someone in the spirit (realm)—either God, the Father, or Satan the deceiver. Choose wisely.

God bless you!

Who Will Supply?

Ever have a need that caused your stomach to turn? You may be feeling that way now. Oftentimes, we turn to family members or friends for assistance, and they may or may not be able to help us.

Relatives and friends have limited resources. God, on the other hand, has unlimited resources. He is also willing and able to supply every one of our needs. As a matter of fact, this is what the Bible says in Philippians 4:19: "And this same God who takes care of me will supply all your needs from his glorious riches, which have been given to us in Christ Jesus."

Who will supply? God will, so live for Him in all your ways. Don't worry about what your circumstances look like. Give it to God, and He will make it all right. Turn to Jesus, the living water, if you truly desire to live. Needs not met should be blamed on an individual's separation from God. God promises to supply all of our needs. I believe Him, and you should too. Stop running to everyone else; run to God instead. He sees your need and, more importantly, He has the ability to fulfill it.

God bless you!

A Good Fear

The Bible tells us we were not given a spirit of fear, yet many people are fearful. Some fears seem ridiculous, you've got to admit—the fear of shaking someone's hand, the fear of going anywhere near the ocean because of sharks, or even the fear of warm water while taking a shower. If you must be fearful, let me tell you something that is worth fearing: you should fear doing evil, wrong, or any ungodly act. The Word of God says in Proverbs 28:14: "Blessed are those who fear to do wrong but the stubborn are headed for serious trouble."

Doing wrong will bring a negative reaction from both God and man, so try your best to do right. No sin goes unpunished, so please keep your sin to a minimum. When we accept what Jesus Christ did on the cross for us over two thousand years ago, it is much easier to live a life of gratitude to Him. To some, His death on the cross was insignificant. How wrong they are! Jesus feared going to the cross. He even asked God the Father to take it away from Him, but because of His love for us, He obeyed the calling on His life.

Christians also have a calling on their lives—that is, to be righteous and holy in Christ Jesus. Is there a good way to see if you are in the right track? Test yourself and be truthful about your fear of doing wrong. If it is no big deal, you have some work to do.

God bless you!

Actions of the Wise

"I didn't mean to do it," said the teenager, watching his friend bleed with bloodstained knife in hand. The good news: the young man didn't die, and his family didn't press charges. Unfortunately, many of these stories don't end this way; most times the end is fatal when weapons are involved due to someone's anger.

As a people with the wisdom of God, we should not allow the blood in our bodies to start boiling. When we get to that point, anything can happen. Let's think things through before we do. The Bible tells us this in Proverbs 13:16: "Wise people think before they act; fools don't and even brag about their foolishness."

In the past, I've heard a hit man bragging about his assignments. How foolish this is to me now knowing the Word of God. Abstain from sin by analyzing everything. Nothing is too great or small that can cause us to fall. Remember to ask yourself: what benefits will come from my actions? Carefully look at what will be gained and honestly consider what could be lost. A divorced man once said that a half-hour adulterous act caused him a lifetime of missing a beautiful wife and two children.

Be wise. Think before you act. Jesus, the righteous judge, is watching.

God bless you!

Hardworking Father

A man or woman who works hard to support his or her family should be honored. Work is a choice we make to accomplish goals, which, in most cases, a paycheck can facilitate. In the spiritual realm of things, Satan and his fallen angels work hard at presenting us with temptations. Glory be to God our Heavenly Father. Our Lord Jesus Christ never stops working, day or night, in our behalf.

The Bible says this in John 5:16–17: "So the Jewish leaders began harassing Jesus for breaking the Sabbath rules. But Jesus replied, 'My Father is always working, and so am I.'"

What a blessing it is to know that God is on the case. No matter what we are facing, we have a hardworking Father who never sleeps working it out for us. All we need to do is open up our hearts sincerely to Him, trust Him, and watch Him work through us. Miracle after miracle, we will be motivated to become more like Him.

Can you see the hand of God working in your life? If not, turn to Him today. Thank Him for all He has done, all He is doing, and all that He will do. He is working for you, so let's get to work for Him.

God bless you!

Sport Fishing

Some people go sport fishing for fun. They don't necessarily catch fish to cook; they say it's just fun to catch and release. The church can learn a thing or two from sport fishing. Let's start with what our Lord Jesus Christ says in Luke 5:10: "Don't be afraid! From now on you'll be fishing for people!"

The church's biggest problem is not catching human fish. It's done regularly. The real problem is how "the fish" are released back into the world. A fisherman is gentle with his catch, removing the fish with care. After which the fish can go produce more fish. The church often strangles new converts with rules, bylaws, and responsibilities that add stress and heavy burdens. No wonder so many fish die on the hook spiritually.

If you are being pressured, or if you are the one applying the pressure, please stop. Ask Jesus to lead your positioning of the saints or the position you are to fill in the church. We, the church, are the people of God in Christ Jesus, not bondage created by a religious system or cult. Who the Son sets free is free indeed.

God bless you!

What Are You Searching For?

Search engines are very popular these days. A recent study shows 180,000,000 visits to one site in a single month. That is some amazing number, but it makes me wonder what those folks were searching for. The Bible tells us in Proverbs 11:27, "If you search for good, you will find favor; but if you search for evil, it will find you!" Isn't that the truth! There are pop-ups out there in cyberspace that are simply outrageous, designed to make us fall.

Please be careful when searching; keep it holy and clean. Perhaps, your problem is not the computer; maybe it's the TV. The same encouragement applies: keep it holy and clean. Search for programs that Jesus can sit beside you and enjoy. You can believe that if Jesus is not by your side, Satan will be asking, "Pass me the popcorn!" If evil ways are in your heart, the devil will always hang out with you. What are evil ways? It is any lifestyle that ignores following the Word of God.

So, in your searching, seek Jesus Christ and His kingdom first, along with all His righteousness. My friend, then and only then can you be totally pleased with what you find.

God bless you!

Genuine Praise

"Praise the Lord," says the psalmist to the world. "Thank you," says the world. Have you ever heard that reply when saying "Praise the Lord" to someone? Or, perhaps, you don't say "Praise the Lord" to anyone.

Genuine praise happens naturally, even outside a controlled environment like church or a Bible study group. While out in public, we should still praise Him without shame. We often need a reminder on giving genuine praise. In Psalm 150:1, 2, and 6 (NLT), David says this: "Praise the Lord! Praise God in his sanctuary; praise Him in His mighty Heaven! Praise Him for His mighty works; praise His unequaled greatness! Let everything that breathes sing praises to the Lord! Praise the Lord!" Our praise should be our lifestyle, not some forced objective. And it won't be genuine if we are not sold out to Jesus Christ and living for Him daily.

So, before you can imitate the psalmist, you must confess your sins to Jesus. Once you've had your own personal experience, then your praises will flow like a river. Others aren't crazy when they praise God nonstop. It's when we aren't praising Him that we look crazy to God. Start praising God today. Make it genuine. God is more than ready to receive it.

God bless you!

God's Highway Is Better
Than the Low Way

It is not popular these days to talk about the last days. Most people are planning for ten, twenty years down the road. Personally, I doubt we will be here that long based on the times we are living in. For those who've accepted Jesus Christ as Lord and Savior and daily lived for Him, they are ready for the rapture or God's Highway. However, most people are focusing on the earthly paradise or the low way. After the rapture happens, just remember that it is better to die than accept the mark of the beast.

Revelation 14:9–12 tells us, "Anyone who worships the beast and his statue or who accepts his mark on the forehead or the hand must drink the wine of God's wrath. And they will be tormented with fire and burning sulfur in the presence of the holy angels and the Lamb. The smoke of their torment rises forever and ever, and they will have no relief day or night, for they have worshipped the beast and his statue and have accepted the mark of his name. Let this encourage God's holy people to endure persecution patiently and remain firm to the end, obeying his commands and trusting in Jesus."

That says it all. Allow these words to take root and grow in your spirit. Enjoy God's highway. See you there.

God bless you!

BMW: Bless My Waiting

I must admit that visiting the doctor for a checkup, filling out some forms, and then being told to sit and wait bother me a little. Some facilities have made me wait forty-five minutes to an hour. I then start to ask myself, "What was the purpose in making an appointment?" The Lord usually tugs at my heart and says, "It's not about you, Trevor. It's all about Jesus!" When we use this perspective, there is a blessing in our waiting.

I love what David says in Psalm 5:3 (NLT): "Listen to my voice in the morning, Lord. Each morning I bring my requests to you and wait expectantly." This lets me know that if we pray with sincere hearts full of faith, we can make requests to God and wait confidently. The beauty of waiting confidently is knowing that your request will be granted to the glory of God. We can enjoy life while we wait and not be stressed out. A lack of faith will steal our blessing while we wait.

Be true in your walk with God. Make your request to Him and be blessed while waiting on a bigger blessing.

God bless you!

Spit It Out

While growing up in Jamaica, we used to eat sugarcane on the street corner after playing soccer. However, the interesting thing about eating sugarcane is that you don't swallow the stalk or "trash." You spit it out. We all knew the juice from the sugarcane was good, but to eat the trash was bad. The same is true of life. We can feed on good things, which give us knowledge, or we can feed on bad things or "trash." As a matter of fact, that is what the Bible says in Proverbs 15:14 (NLT): "A wise person is hungry for knowledge, while the fool feeds on trash."

Don't be foolish in life. You only have one go at it to make a good impression on God. Spit out the trash. Embrace wisdom, knowledge, and understanding according to God's Word. Some people are not only trash talkers but also trash compactors—meaning they store lots of negativity. Don't feed your spirit with it or pay attention to what those friends are saying. Know this: if our words and actions don't glorify God, they glorify Satan.

Don't give the devil the opportunity to talk trash about you to God the Father as he did in Job 1. Allow God to boast about you as He boasted about Job. Spit out life's trash today.

God bless you!

Staying Pure

Imagine a new mom and her hungry infant. She pumps milk for the baby in a bottle and then adds one drop of black ink to it, mixes it up, and gives it to the baby.

I apologize if that story turns your stomach, but that is what our Heavenly Father faces every day. His children defile themselves daily by not obeying His Word. This really upsets His stomach. This is what the Bible says in Psalm 119:9: "How can a young person stay pure? By obeying your word."

How serious are you about staying pure? You may say, "I am not pure, so how can I stay pure?" It's easy to get there. Just repeat this payer: "Lord God, I confess I am a sinner. Please forgive me of my sins. Wash me clean and make me pure. Keep me in your word and help me to live for you in Jesus's name. Amen."

My friend, if you said that prayer from your heart, you are now pure. Your only challenge now is to stay pure. Get God's Word in you, and it will push the things of this world out of you. Staying pure is a choice; make it today.

God bless you!

College Rules

Everywhere we go, there are rules to abide by, and college is no exception. In order to make it in college, one must be a self-starter and self-reliant to a certain degree. One rule I think ought to be posted on the wall of every college should be, "Each student must be a leader in thought and in deed." I love that; after all, Mom and Dad don't live on college campus with their children.

Taking initiative and leadership are very important not only in college but also in everyday life. The Bible says this in Proverbs 12:24: "Work hard and become a leader, be lazy and become a slave." Something to keep in mind: Anyone who refuses to lead their life under the guidance of the Holy Spirit will be a slave to sin and to Satan. Let's implement this college rule by being leaders in thought and deed. When the devil brings thoughts to mind, rebuke him in Jesus's name. It takes a leader to declare war on Satan. Anyone refusing to lead will become Satan's slave. The thought of slavery does not sit well with me, so I choose to follow the Holy Spirit's lead down the straight and narrow path.

Take back your life from the devil today and give it to Jesus. That's what a true leader does.

God bless you!

A Heart Free from Hanging

We, as human beings, encounter many opportunities to get angry with others. Although it may happen, we must prayerfully be sure we don't stay angry for long because anger causes evil to fester in our hearts. In the book of Esther, King Xerxes's right-hand man, Haman, got angry with Mordecai for not bowing down to him. Haman's anger turned into hatred not only for Mordecai but also for the entire Jewish race. Haman went to the king and received permission to wipe out the Jews on a set date. However, that date wasn't soon enough for Haman, so he erected a pole to hang Mordecai on.

How many people do we hang in our hearts? My friends, make sure your heart is free from hanging others. You don't want to end up like Haman. Esther 7:9 says, "Then Harbona, one of the king's eunuchs, said, 'Haman has set up a sharpened pole that stands seventy five feet tall in his own courtyard. He intended to use it to impale Mordecai, the man who saved the king from assassination.' 'Then impale Haman on it!' the king ordered." Haman hanged Mordecai in his heart, but Haman ended up dying physically for it. Don't lose your blessing due to hanging in your heart. Forgive today and live. If you are digging a hole for an enemy, you'd better dig two—the other, for you. The way of love is better.

God bless you!

The Road

In the natural way of thinking, most people would rather choose the road with least resistance when traveling to their destination. If you are driving down a local road and the potholes are overwhelming, you might turn off and head to a highway if it's available. That reaction may work in the natural, but it wouldn't be beneficial in the spiritual.

The Bible says in Matthew 7:13–14 (NLT), "You can enter God's kingdom only through the narrow gate. The highway to hell is broad, and its gate is wide for the many who choose the easy way. But the gateway to life is very narrow, and the road is difficult and only a few ever find it."

The road less traveled should be the road more desired. So, what's along the narrow road? Confession of sin, being forgiving, receiving forgiveness, holiness, righteousness, love, grace, mercy, long suffering with Christ, peace in the midst of the storm, mountains, valleys, and, through it all, the confident assurance that all things are working together for the good of those who love God and are called according to His purpose. Which road are you on today? If it is hell's highway, exit before you crash and burn. The road to life is much better.

God bless you!

Standing Firm in the Lord

How great it is to see fellow Christians you haven't seen in years and hear them say, "Praise the Lord! How are you?" Some believers respond, "I'm standing firm in the Lord!" Although my usual response is, "I'm truly blessed and highly favored," I must admit that I love standing firm in the Lord as well. This tells me that the individual is still fighting the good fight of faith.

The apostle Paul was encouraged by the church in Thessalonica when he wrote this in 1 Thessalonians 3:7–8 (NLT): So we have been greatly encouraged in the midst of our troubles and suffering, dear brothers and sisters, because you have remained strong in your faith. It gives us new life to know that you are standing firm in the Lord."

Let's be an encouragement in the way we live our lives by showing others we are standing firm. Our daily hymn should be "On Christ the Solid Rock I Stand (All Other Ground Is Sinking Sand)."

When we consider the alternative and where it ends, standing firm in the Lord should be a lot easier to do. Don't lose ground. Soon a reward will be yours for your faithfulness. Keep on standing.

God bless you!

Before the Sun Goes Down

Way back before light fixtures were available, people had to complete all they needed to accomplish before the sun goes down. That scenario is not so bad because in most cases they could pick up where they left off on the following day.

However, there's a more severe scenario—when people traveled in those days, they would try their best to make it into a town before the sun goes down. The reason is simply this: sleeping out in the desert could mean a poisonous snake bite.

"Before the sun goes down..." The same is true for today. The Bible says this in Ephesians 4:26–27: "And don't sin by letting anger control you. Don't let the sun go down while you are still angry. For anger gives a foothold to the devil."

If you go to sleep with anger, be careful; the snake is ready to bite. If you are angry with someone, lovingly confront them. Work it out. If they choose not to work it out, forgive them and move on. We are not responsible for the actions of others, but we must give an account for ours. Work while it is daylight. Rid yourself of anger.

God bless you!

Newborn Spiritual Babies

Everyone loves a newborn baby. His or her race or size doesn't seem to matter, newborns are adorable! Newborns have a hunger and a thirst for milk. They kick, scream, cry, and even grab to get it. I wish newborn spiritual babies had the same zeal for spiritual milk. The Bible says this in 1 Peter 2:1–3: "So get rid of all evil behavior. Be done with all deceit, hypocrisy, jealousy, and all unkind speech. Like newborn babies, you must crave pure spiritual milk so that you will grow into a full experience of salvation. Cry out for this nourishment, now that you have had a taste of the Lord's kindness."

Peter said new believers should crave this spiritual milk. This means do whatever it takes to hear the Word. Most "newborn" Christians fail because they stop hearing the Word (or getting the real Word) in church, stop reading the Bible, or stop praying. Don't be fooled. The devil is angry that you gave your life to the Lord. Many demons have been dispatched to get you back into the world. Natural newborns need milk daily until they can eat chewable food. Spiritual newborns must, with the help of God, rid themselves of evil lifestyles and cling to righteousness. The more we walk with the Lord, the more we grow. Sometimes we need to take a lesson from a baby in order to get the Word.

God bless you!

He Has Done Great Things

When you think of greatness, what comes to mind? Winning a pro sport championship? Becoming the CEO of a Fortune 500 company or the president of a nation? All those are great, but here's another to add to the list: how about having been chosen to give birth to the Messiah, Jesus Christ? A young virgin girl named Mary was chosen for such a great yet humbling task. In Luke 1:49, Mary sang this song of praise: "For the Mighty One is holy, and He has done great things for me."

I sing with Mary today because of what Jesus was born to accomplish. The Father has truly done great things for me and all who receive the free gift of salvation offered through Jesus Christ. Not accepting Jesus Christ as Lord and Savior before one dies disqualifies that individual from partaking of the eternally great thing that God has done. Many people celebrate Christmas without acknowledging the reason for the season. It's not just a day to receive presents; it's a celebration of the fact that our Savior was born. Make this Christmas extra special and accept the gift of salvation that Jesus came to earth to bring to you. When you do, your name will be registered as a citizen of heaven. Then, follow His lead each day. In my opinion, friend, that is the greatest thing ever.

God bless you!

Ready to Learn

Every day that we're alive, we should be learning something new. Our brains are designed to receive new data on a daily basis, but the question is, are you ready to learn? The Word of God is designed to educate and motivate us in righteousness in learning the ways of God the Father and our Lord Jesus Christ. Learning His ways, however, takes discipline.

A powerful verse that says just that is Proverbs 12:1: "To learn you must love discipline; it is stupid to hate correction." Discipline and correction are a part of the learning process, so there is nothing wrong if you make a mistake. Many Christians fall away from the church because they've sinned against God. News flash: everyone sins against God in some form or another. The key thing is to not keep sinning against God.

Accept biblical correction. Discipline yourself in Bible reading, bible study, church attendance, and fellowship. These simple steps let God know that you are ready to learn. He will then reveal to you the mysteries that are hidden in his Word. You have the green light now, so learn.

God bless you!

Looking Forward to It

I look forward to dining in my favorite restaurant. I can already taste the food an hour before getting there.

Unlike greedy persons such as myself, others look forward to vacations, job promotions, church, Bible study, or just spending time with family. While these are all good, they will soon be forgotten. This is what the Bible says in Isaiah 65:17: "Look! I am creating new heavens and a new Earth, and no one will even think about the old ones anymore."

When we get to heaven, it will blow our minds. Now that is what I'm looking forward to. How about you, my friend? Have you made your entrance into heaven a priority? Be careful in just looking forward to the things of this world. They often carry a false guarantee. However, the authenticity of heaven is real. All who make it there are secure for all eternity.

Take a moment to analyze your life and see just what it is you are really looking forward to. My friendly advice: make heaven the number one on your list and live in such a way that complements your decision.

God bless you!

Get Your House in Order

There's a knock on the door.

"Who is it?" asks Sister Evelyn.

"It's Pastor and First Lady Brown."

"Oh! Just a minute!" replies Sister Evelyn. Five minutes later after an emergency cleanup, she finally opens the door.

Many are guilty of the same crime—not putting their house in order until a visitor arrives, but let's pray our spirit man isn't like that. The Bible tells us this in Luke 12:35–36: "Be dressed for service and keep your lamps burning, as though you were waiting for your master to return from the wedding feast. Then you will be ready to open the door and let Him in the moment he arrives and knocks."

My friends, Jesus will come at an hour when you least expect it, so get your spiritual house in order. Stop saying you need to get right and just get right already. God is tired of supposed-to-be Christians playing Russian Roulette with their eternity. Even if the Lord tarries a few more days, weeks, or months, an individual can still pass away from something else. Trust the Word of God. Eternity is a long time to pay for something that can be rectified today. Get your house in order by following God's order.

God bless you!

Do You Pass Your Daily Exam?

Students in junior high, high school, and college study really hard to pass exams. They know that they will be graded for what they do when presented with the test papers.

Notice I didn't say "For what they know" because we may know right and still do wrong. That's how it is with mankind. We know deep in our hearts that lying, stealing, killing, unforgiveness, cursing, and things of that nature are wrong. However, people continue to do so without remorse and fail their daily exam.

The Bible says this in Psalm 11:4: "But the Lord is in His holy temple; the Lord still rules from heaven. He watches everyone closely, examining every person on earth."

Pass your exams with flying colors. The Lord is watching. Study the Bible and ask God to reveal His wonderful truths to you. Research who Jesus is, the crossing of the Red Sea, Sodom and Gomorrah, and other biblical events of the past that will make you more aware of biblical events to come. In other words, become a believer and have your actions reflect that. Each and every day, we should seek to get an A from His majesty.

God bless you!

It's Coming Back

Remember a time when life was easy? When Mom and Dad took care of everything? When you had no bills to think of and your only problem was that not enough time was spent at the playground?

As an adult, many continue to be blessed with good health, finances, etc. Perhaps, due to variable circumstances, our good lives seem to have vanished, and struggling is now in effect. For the believer in Christ, I have this encouragement: your blessing is coming back. When the children of Israel played around with God, the Ark of the Covenant was captured. However, the enemy cannot keep what doesn't belong to Him without turmoil. The Bible tells us this in 1 Samuel 6:1–2: "The Ark of the Lord remained in Philistine territory seven months in all. Then the Philistines called in their priests and diviners and asked them, 'What should we do about the Ark of the Lord? Tell us how to return it to its own country.'"

For the children of Israel, when the ark was with them, that meant God was present with them. Without the ark, they had no confidence, joy, or hope. If you've been robbed by the enemy, have no fear. Hold on to Jesus. He has angels dispatched to fight on your behalf. Whether it's a health issue, relationship issue, or even finances, it's coming back. Walk by faith. Believe that God will do it for you. For some, it is now, and others when we get to heaven, but it's coming back.

God bless you!

Don't Let Go of God

We often throw away things that are not valuable to us. They aren't necessarily things that are old; some have great sentimental value. There seems to be a trend now—individuals trade in a pure relationship with God for a watered-down version.

We need to stop and look at what God did for us, His people. This is what the Bible says in Leviticus 26:13: "I am the Lord your God, who brought you out of the land of Egypt so you would no longer be their slaves. I broke the yoke of slavery from your neck so you can walk with your heads held high."

Let's remember we have liberty, freedom, and salvation with God. Don't give those up for limitations in greatness, slavery, and damnation. Hold on with all your might. I know it's difficult at times, but keep in mind that you have an enemy, Satan, who is working hard to kill you. Don't give up on God. He won't give up on you. Talk with Him daily in prayer. Ask Him to forgive your sins and direct your path. He will do it for you. He loves us more than we love ourselves. He's brought us through many trials and will continue to carry us all the way to heaven. Don't let go.

God bless you!

The Great Freeze

There are stories in the Bible that wow us. Jesus walking on the water, Moses parting the Red Sea, and Lazarus being raised from the dead are all very fascinating stories. However, there's another story we really need to take a look at as many Christians today find themselves lost in the past. The Bible says this in Genesis 19:26: "But Lot's wife looked back as she was following behind him, and she turned into a pillar of salt." The reason Lot's wife was following behind is because she didn't want to leave Sodom in the first place. Her heart was still there. It caused her to look back and experience a great freeze by salt.

Many Christians today are at risk of losing their salvation because they keep going back to their past lives. Our old familiar ways of living are very dangerous, and the only solution is to ask God for a new heart. When God performs a heart surgery on us and we receive His Holy Spirit with a willingness to follow, then we are on our way. We will escape the great freeze of not progressing in our relationships—financially or physically. Let's trust God for our future and stay out of the rearview mirror. Perform a self-analysis. If you find yourself thinking about the past way too often, you may be frozen. Let it go and then go forth with Jesus.

God bless you!

Dancing King

Lots of folks love to dance, don't they? I didn't say lots of folks are good at dancing, but they still love to dance. There is absolutely nothing wrong with making a few moves to glorify God. I dance because I have salvation. That fact alone is all the reason I need

The Ark of the Covenant represented the presence of God, so when the Israelites brought it to Jerusalem, they partied hard. The Bible says this in 2 Samuel 6:13–14: "After the men who were carrying the Ark of the Lord had gone six steps, David sacrificed a bull and a fattened calf. And David danced before the Lord with all his might, wearing a priestly garment." Can you imagine the king dancing with all his might? Churches today are lacking that genuine joy of being in the Lord's presence.

Let's start dancing for the Lord—in church, our homes, in the streets, at the parks, anywhere the Lord leads us. There is a great blessing attached to glorifying God in our dancing, so get to stepping! We used to dance for the devil, didn't we? Let's change allegiance and dance like the king for the King of kings.

God bless you!

Don't Complicate It

The Gospel of Jesus Christ is often complicated by those teaching it. Please be reminded that Jesus didn't come to earth to burden us with doctrine. Jesus came to show us how to love and be loved. Let's not lose sight on what love is. Love is patient, kind, not rude or irritable, and does not demand its own way.

My friends, if we exercise love, then we've got it made. When we develop love in action, then we will live out the scriptures. Matthew 7:12: "Do to others whatever you would like them to do to you. This is the essence of all that is taught in the law and the prophets."

We can get caught in the trap of religion if we lose focus on our relationships. Jesus focused on relationships, and so should we. The way we walk and talk should reflect Christ. Treat people with love and respect just as you would like them to treat you. Read the Word of God for yourself and keep in mind that if we don't love others, God is not leading us because God is love.

Don't complicate the Gospel. Embrace and elevate it. God will see us through as we do what we are called to do.

God bless you!

It's Waived, Go and Sin No More

The world is brutal to the accused in most cases. Guilty or not once accused, one will face many trials. Whether one confesses or is proven guilty, wouldn't he still have to pay the price for his crime? That is how it works naturally, but what about spiritually?

There was a woman caught in the very act of adultery, and the Law of Moses stated such a woman should be stoned to death. Let's take a look at what Jesus said in John 8:7–11: "They kept demanding an answer, so he stood up again and said, 'All right, but let the one who has never sinned throw the first stone!' When the accusers heard this, they slipped away one by one...Then Jesus stood up again and said to the woman, 'Where are your accusers? Didn't even one of them condemn you?' 'No, Lord,' she said. And Jesus said, 'Neither do I. Go and sin no more.'"

All of her penalties were waived with a warning. Please keep in mind that if we continue to sin after confessing our sins, then our previous forgiven sins are back on the map. It's like this: sin begets sin and more sin. Don't give the devil a portal to revive your waived penalties. Go and sin no more and then you will smile with Jesus for sure.

God bless you!

Who Is Your Master?

Who is the master of your life? Some are quick to say, "I have no master," or "I am my own master." Let me lovingly correct those with that mindset and let them know that we all serve a master. The way we live our lives lets us know who our master is. If someone lies, steals, kills, fornicates, hates, envies, or the like, then Satan is their master. There is no mistaken identity there; it is what it is. However, if someone who truly loves—even an enemy—is forgiving, patient, kind, accepts Jesus Christ as Lord and Savior, and then lives for Him, then God the Almighty is their master.

David says this in Psalm 16:2: "I said to the Lord, 'You are my master! Every good thing I have comes from you.'" It is such a great feeling to know that my master, the creator of the universe, gives me good things. My old master, Satan, desired to kill me and still does because that is his purpose here on earth. Who is your master? If you can honestly say, "God the Father," well, congratulations! If Satan is your master, based on biblical guidelines, please consider changing allegiance before this life is over. Change your expectations from eternal death to eternal life. It is free to us because Jesus paid the price. Allow Jesus to be your master.

God bless you!

The Very Best Memorial

When we hear the word *memorial*, most automatically assume someone has died. While true in the most common use of the word, it also means "anything meant to help people remember a person, event, etc." The children of Israel were delivered from the hand of Pharaoh by God's miracles. God then placed them in the land of Canaan where they defeated all their enemies, and so the tribes on the Eastern side of the Jordan River built a memorial to worship God. The Bible tells us this in Joshua 22:26–28 (NLT): "So we decided to build the altar, not for burnt offerings or sacrifices, but as a memorial. It will remind our descendants and your descendants that we, too, have the right to worship the Lord at His sanctuary with our burnt offerings, sacrifices and peace offerings. Then your descendants will not be able to say to ours, 'You have no claim to the Lord.'"

What a powerful memorial to have the right to worship the Lord. We, as Christians, enjoy a memorial as well: Jesus died and was raised on the third day. We have an empty cross, a memorial to worship God because of what Jesus did for our salvation. The question is: do we use our memorial and actually worship, or do we ignore it? When we commemorate what Jesus did for us and live a life of worship toward Him, well, that's the very best memorial.

God bless you!

Small Things with Big Results

Some individuals are masters of excuses, believing they have little resources so nothing great can be accomplished. Let me encourage you that being small in size or having little resources should not be a hindrance to your accomplishing great things. Partner with Jesus and see really great things derive from humble beginnings.

Before David was king, he was a shepherd boy who worked really hard. When his older brothers were home ready to feast, David remained in the fields. David had a heart to serve, and God promoted him from a shepherd of flocks to king of Israel.

Proverbs 6:6–8 provides another good example, which says: "Take a lesson from the ants, you lazybones. Learn from their ways and become wise! Though they have no prince or governor or ruler to make them work, they labor hard all summer, gathering food for the winter." Talk about big results from a small insect. Some people refuse to work a week, let alone the entire summer. It all boils down to perspective, so here is one for you: to build a mountain, it is best to start with an anthill. Seek guidance from God and build each day. Before you know it, things will be great. Keep the faith no matter how small you may feel. To Jesus Christ, you are a big deal.

God bless you!

The Ultimate Blasphemy

I've heard someone say, "I have blasphemed against the Holy Spirit, so I am on my way to hell. There is no use in trying to get forgiveness from God." You would be surprised at the number of people Satan has told that lie to and who believe it. First of all, the mere fact that someone acknowledges that they've blasphemed against the Holy Spirit lets me know that there is a certain level of conviction.

Jesus says this in Matthew 12:31: "So I tell you, every sin and blasphemy can be forgiven—except blasphemy against the Holy Spirit, which will never be forgiven." The Pharisees had just accused Jesus of casting out a demon by using power from Satan. Jesus is highly annoyed when the power of God through the Holy Spirit is undermined. Keep in mind that on the day Jesus was raptured, He said that when the Holy Spirit comes, we would have power to tell this good news (Acts 1:8).

So, in essence, it's all about power of the Holy Spirit and His ability to save the lost. The ultimate blasphemy against the Holy Spirit is to deny or reduce His power to some cosmic force, who is not at all God. Look into this matter. Truly become saved, making sure the Holy Spirit is leading your life daily. He is the only one who knows the way to heaven. To die without the Holy Spirit is blasphemy you cannot repent of. If you are breathing, you can repent.

God bless you!

Promissory Note

Has anyone you know said, "I promise you," lately? A verbal promise is so common these days, like yes and no. However, a promissory note is different. Now you have your verbal promise in writing, signed by you just in case you decide to have voluntary amnesia. Many people go to church and make promises they cannot keep. Please don't do that. The Bible says this in Ecclesiastes 5:1–2: (NLT) "As you enter the house of God, keep your ears open and your mouth shut. It is evil to make mindless offerings to God. Don't make rash promises, and don't be hasty in bringing matters before God. After all, God is in Heaven, and you are here on Earth. So let your words be few."

Think about your circumstances before promising God. When you promise God that you'll do or not do something, you sign a promissory note on your heart. To break that promise or to tear up the note leads to a broken and torn heart, which isn't good at all. The promises God made to us are true. Jesus Christ said, "Come unto me all who labor and are heavy laden I will give you rest." I answered that call many years ago and can honestly say I have been resting in Christ Jesus. My only prerequisite was to promise I will do my best in living for Him. Consider all you have to gain or lose and make your choice today. Always do your best to honor your promises.

God bless you!

Fully Loaded

Every individual is fully loaded with one spirit or another. The way we live our lives will let us know which spirit we are full of. There is a great story in Acts 16 that will help me explain this point. Acts 16:16–18 says this: "One day as we were going down to the place of prayer, we met a demon-possessed slave girl. She was a fortune-teller who earned a lot of money for her masters. She followed Paul and the rest of us, shouting, 'These men are servants of the Most High God, and they have come to tell you how to be saved.' This went on day after day until Paul got so exasperated that he turned and said to the demon within her, 'I command you in the name of Jesus Christ to come out of her.' And instantly it left her."

What a contrast! The slave girl was full of demons, and Paul was fully loaded with the Holy Spirit. Paul rebuked the demon and helped the young girl, but what about us today? Have we become exasperated with our evil influences yet? If we have, we will desire to change ammunition and start fighting the real enemy. Switch sides. Become fully loaded with the spirit of God. Don't think it's a joke or insignificant. We only get one shot at this life, so live right. Each individual will either enhance or fight against the Kingdom of God. Which will you do?

God bless you!

Graduating Class

Graduation is a very exciting time for students and for teachers alike—perhaps, even more for the teacher who may be looking forward to the break.

There's an upcoming graduation that will be the most important of all. Graduation from this earth! Whether or not you're aware, we all must graduate from this earth one day or another. Jesus says this in Luke 12:35–38: "Be dressed for service and keep your lamps burning, He may come in the middle of the night or just before dawn. But whenever He comes, he will reward the servants who are ready." During an earthly graduation, we must be dressed in cap and gown. The same is true for our spiritual graduation. We must be dressed in salvation, which is our cap or helmet. We can then put on righteousness, truth, and peace while living out the sword of the spirit, which is the Word of God.

Don't be caught undressed when you die or when the rapture occurs. Get dressed now. Don't wait until tomorrow; tomorrow is not guaranteed to anyone. Jesus is a master fashion designer. Come to Him as you are. He will wash you clean and dress you for His special graduating class. Ask yourself: why just graduate when you can graduate with honors?

God bless you!

Restorer of Fine Things

Some people have the special gift of restoration. I've seen old model cars that were once candidates for the junkyard restored to being brand-new. God gave this gift of restoration to those mechanics and body shop specialists.

However, I must elaborate on a more important matter, and that is the restoration of a soul. The Bible says this in James 5:19–20: "My dear brothers and sisters, if someone among you wanders away from the truth and is brought back, you can be sure that whoever brings the sinner back will save that person from death and bring about the forgiveness of many sins."

Along this Christian journey, many believers tend to stray off the straight and narrow path. It is up to us, who are strong in the Lord, to help restore the finer things in these strayed individuals—righteousness, holiness, truthfulness, forgiveness, faithfulness, and love. Don't just label someone lost forever without trying to revive their soul. Should an individual refuse to listen, don't lose faith. Keep praying, and one day, God-willing, they will confess. Keep a restoration mindset for believers gone astray. If you're reading this and you've gone astray, remember Jesus loves you and He wants you back home. May the Holy Spirit restore you today.

God bless you!

From a Trap to Protection

Traps are set daily by the evil one for people to fall into. While we must face the facts about this, protection in God is another fact. The real question is how long are we willing to fall, to fail, to be abused, to be used, or to just lose?

David realized the devil's trap through his enemies. This was his prayer in Psalm 31:4: "Pull me from the trap my enemies set for me, for I find protection in you alone." Under the protection of the Almighty God is a much better place to be. We are blessed with life when we are created, but the enemy often leads us astray until we get hip to his game and call on Jesus's name. Whoever calls on the name of the Lord with a sincere heart will be saved, and not lip service but heart service.

If you are sick and tired of failure and everything else that the devil has to offer, you can turn to Jesus for real protection. When your soul is protected in God, you have Heaven to look forward to. The earthly traps can be seen and sidestepped. In the battle of where we'll spend eternity, don't give the enemy and his traps the victory. Jesus is calling to save and protect you. Answer Him. Live for Him.

God bless you!

Truly Satisfy Your Spirit

We live in a fast-paced world, with highways, Internet, microwaves, and more. Because we want satisfaction right now, businesses use the motto, "Satisfaction guaranteed," so that we're drawn to them. Money often becomes a priority over God, although I have never seen a Brink's truck following a hearse.

This is what the Bible says in Psalm 39:6: "We are merely moving shadows, and all our busy rushing ends in nothing. We heap up wealth, not knowing who will spend it." My friends, please understand that our spirit man never dies. Our physical bodies get old and die unexpectedly. Our spirits want to be satisfied in God. Satisfying the flesh with money, cars, clothing, jewelry, relationships, and the like is poor in comparison to a right relationship with Jesus Christ. This is why many wealthy people commit suicide. Money cannot fill the void in their hearts or give them a peaceful spirit.

A word of advice: invest in your future by truly satisfying your spirit. Accept the Spirit of Jesus Christ also known as the Holy Spirit. When you do, He will remove the junk and replace it with top-quality merchandise. The return on your investment will be out of this world. Allow the Holy Spirit to lead you, thus, truly satisfying your spirit. Why not start today?

God bless you!

Important Insurance

Every once in a while, the Holy Spirit instructs me to write words that may seem a bit harsh. This is one of those times. To get one's point across is not always easy, so please pay close attention while you read. Insurance policies are a part of everyday life. We need car insurance to drive legally, health insurance, which pays at least half of our medical bills, and renter's or homeowner's insurance, which protects us from damage or theft. There is also another insurance that is very important. Actually, I can say it is the most important insurance there is. It is to have your name written in the Lamb's Book of Life.

The Bible says this in Revelation 20:15: "And anyone whose name was not found recorded in the Book of Life was thrown into the lake of fire." If you have not read Revelations 20:11–15, I strongly advise that you do. It pertains to every human being who ever lived. You see, we will all be judged by God. There will be no parole. If sentenced to the Lake of Fire, it is forever burning, and because we all receive a body that will not physically die, individuals will be tormented forever. It is not by chance that you are reading this. God wants to get a message through to you. I encourage you to listen to Him. Repent and be baptized. Sign the contract and receive the most important insurance known to man—your name entered in the Book of Life.

God bless you!

It's No Big Deal

A friend of mine told me that he and a business partner lost more than two hundred fifty million dollars of investor's money in the stock market decline in the year 2000. He also lost over twenty-five million dollars of his own personal net worth in that market collapse. Upon arrival to his office, he found that his partner committed suicide with a gun. He was about to do the same, but the phone kept ringing and ringing. He answered the phone, and it was his mother saying, "Don't do anything crazy. God loves you and will use you!" She told him to read Psalm 27 and then to come over and see her. He did.

This is a true story, and I've heard of many others who lost it all and killed themselves. That is exactly what the devil wants, but God has more in store if you wait on Him. Job lost everything in one day—money, children, status, among others. But let's take a look at his response in Job 1:20–21: "Job stood up and tore his robe in grief. Then he shaved his head and fell to the ground to worship. He said, 'I came naked from my mother's womb, and I will be naked when I leave. The Lord gave me what I had, and the Lord has taken it away. Praise the name of the Lord!'"

Are you able to worship when calamity strikes? If Jesus is your Lord and Savior, it's no big deal when trouble comes. He promises to see us through. Trust in Him. Repent of your sins today. Don't delay.

God bless you!

Worship the Holy One

"Sweetheart, I worship the very ground you walk on," says the young man to a new girlfriend. However, in trying to score brownie points with another human being, some sin against God. We were created to worship, but sadly many direct their worship to a person, place, or thing, having no eternal rewards.

The word *worship* really means "worth ship," or in other words, "worthy of praises given." No one else is deserving of worship but the Holy One. He tells us this in Exodus 20:3–4: "You must not have any other God but me. You must not make for yourself an idol of any kind or an image of anything in the heavens or on the earth or in the sea. You must not bow down to them or worship them, for I, the Lord your God, am a jealous God who will not tolerate your affection for any other gods." Anything we worship becomes our god. When we worship the Holy One, we make deposits into our heavenly bank accounts. Likewise, when we worship idols, we make withdrawals from our heavenly bank account.

A word of advice: don't allow your account in heaven to close because you chose to worship self, flesh, or money. Worship the Holy One! If you haven't yet opened a heavenly bank account, repent of your sins today. Accept Jesus Christ as Lord and Savior. Live a lifestyle of worship to the Holy One.

God bless you!

Who Is Your Carpenter?

The Home Depot promotes that homeowners do things themselves. Many have tried to build things and failed, while others have been successful. The key thing we must remember when building is to have a good solid foundation.

Let me suggest Jesus Christ as your foundation. Once you've surrendered your life to Him, your spiritual home is on its way. Next, remain in Him, and He will qualify as your carpenter. The peace of mind this brings is phenomenal, my friend. The Bible says this in Psalm 127:1 (NLT): "Unless the Lord builds a house, the work of the builders is wasted. Unless the Lord protects a city, guarding it with sentries will do no good."

Many people fail in life because they choose to build on their own without the Lord. Don't follow the wrong example. Turn to God while you still can. Start building your spiritual home now. Enjoy a peace that surpasseth all understanding here on Earth and an eternally blessed life with Christ among other true believers. Don't allow the devil to continue as your carpenter. Fire him today and start building with Jesus right away.

God bless you!

Lost Dog

I have a T-shirt that reads: D.O.G. Below that: Depend On God. Many believers have strayed from this way of living and have taken life issues into their own hands. Even after continuous failure, people don't realize that they have lost their D.O.G. (Dependency on God).

The Bible says in Psalm 62:7–8: "My victory and honor come from God alone. He is my refuge, a rock where no enemy can reach me. O my people, trust in Him at all times. Pour our your heart to Him, for God is our refuge."

The psalmist is absolutely right; we can depend on God. Always remember, man will fail at one point or another, but God never fails. Have you tasted and seen how good He is (Psalm 34:8)? If not, repent of your sins and invite Jesus Christ into your life as Lord and Savior. Depend on God, and you'll see that He delivers right on time. Don't lose your D.O.G. Keep it active and experience life to the fullest through Jesus Christ. Depend on God. You'll be glad you did.

God bless you!

Can't Find Your Joy?

Peace and joy are promised to the believer. Oftentimes though, believers try to do too much instead of allowing God to have His way. This problem, which starts small in most cases, can quickly become so large that they fail to nourish their salvation. Living each day to please the flesh and not the spirit man is a very dangerous way to live. The enemy knows that when believers are extremely busy, it takes away from time spent with the Lord. Pay close attention to your daily schedule. Extremely busy people oftentimes lose their joy in the mix of things. David says this in Psalm 51:12: "Restore to me the joy of your salvation, and make me willing to obey you." Obedience to God brings true joy. It is vital to read the Word so that we may obey it.

If we are feeling distant from God, guess who moved? We did. We've moved away from true joy and peace, not the kind the world gives—conditional and based on status. If you can't find your joy, don't look any further. Turn to Jesus. Confess or rededicate your life to Him today. Pray as David prayed: "Restore the joy of my salvation!" God did not create us to be stressed and depressed every day. Allow joy to come your way.

God bless you!

What Songs Are You Singing?

When I think of songs I used to sing back in the day, I can't believe it! Boy, was I out there. Perhaps, you feel the same way about back in the day, or maybe you are still out there. Nonetheless, we cannot change the past, but we can write the future. If we must sing, why not sing songs of praise? When we surrender our lives to God by accepting salvation through Jesus Christ, there's supposed to be changes within us. One of those changes should be how we entertain ourselves through the music we listen to and sing.

The Bible says this in Psalm 40:3: He has given me a new song to sing, a hymn of praise to our God. Many will see what He has done and be amazed. They will put their trust in the Lord."

This statement is so true. I have friends who know of the unholy songs I used to sing, but when they hear what I sing now, they are truly amazed. I also have friends who've given their lives to Jesus due to my testimony and the new songs I sing. Keep in mind that when you sing a new song that glorifies God, you never know who may hear you and put their trust in God. What are you singing? Sing songs that glorify the King.

God bless you!

It's Going to Turn

It's sometimes hard to see the light at the end of the tunnel in the face of many dark trials. The children of Israel were faced with annihilation from Persia and Media. However, God intervened and turned things around, saving the lives of the Israelites. This event led Mordecai to instill the Festival of Purim. Esther 9:22 says this: "He told them to celebrate these days with feasting and gladness and by giving gifts of food to each other and presents to the poor. This would commemorate a time when the Jews gained relief from their enemies, when their sorrow was turned into gladness and their mourning into joy."

Maybe you are faced with major difficulties right now—relationships, finances, or life-threatening health issues. I dare you to trust God. Lay it all at the foot of the cross. Begin a three-day fast as Israel did in the book of Esther (chapter 4, verse 16) and watch God turn things around. Stop complaining and start praying. Show God that you truly depend on Him and Him alone. It's going to turn. Turn your fears to faith, and God, through His Son, Jesus Christ, will make you great.

God bless you!

Veteran's Affairs

Having served four years in the United States Navy, I learned a thing or two about following orders. Once enlisted, you've signed over your right to do as you please to the government. You've agreed to be called upon at any time to do anything necessary for the country's well-being. The same is true for the born-again believer. We've surrendered our lives to the Lord, and we're supposed to follow His lead. Make no mistake about this, unless you are enlisted in the Lord's army. He will not share certain important information with you.

I love this story in Joshua 5:13–14: "Joshua went up to him and demanded, 'Are you friend or foe?' 'Neither one,' he replied. 'I am the commander of the Lord's army.' At this, Joshua fell with his face to the ground in reverence. 'I am at your command,' Joshua said. 'What do you want your servant to do?'" Now there's a true veteran in God's army. How do we measure up? As enlisted individuals in the Lord's army, we may be called upon to leave our comfort zone and do something outside the ordinary. We have to fight the enemy's temptations daily. I am talking about getting out of the box—going into the mission field for evangelism, saying "Praise the Lord" to everyone you come in contact with, forgiving individuals who hurt you...the list goes on. Don't think about it; just do it. The enlisted follow the general without asking where every step leads. Follow Christ.

God bless you!

Superman or the Lord's Man

So, who is the real man of steel? Is it Superman? Is it Iron Man? The world views strength very differently from the way God views it. For instance, when we see a bodybuilder with muscles everywhere, we say he's a strong person. However, back in the day, if we'd taken a look at Samson, we wouldn't have thought he was so strong because he wasn't a bodybuilder. What made him strong was the Spirit of the Lord.

The Bible says this in Judges 15:14–15: "As Samson arrived at Lehi, the Philistines came shouting in triumph. But the Spirit of the Lord came powerfully upon Samson, and he snapped the ropes on his arms as if they were burnt strands of flax, and they fell from his wrists. Then he found the jawbone of a recently killed donkey. He picked it up and killed 1,000 Philistines with it." Imagine how strong we believers are when the Spirit of the Lord is upon us. We can speak to sickness and have it be gone. We can cast out demons from our lives and the lives of our loved ones. We can pray for the salvation of others and see them become saved. God used Samson to execute judgment on the Philistines.

What is your calling, man or woman of God? I suggest you earnestly pray about it and allow the Spirit of God to lead you in all power to accomplish His will.

God bless you!

What God Says About Us

It doesn't take much for someone's name to be dragged through the mud. I have decided that it makes no sense to undermine the Word of God in order to please people, the reason being that no matter what you do for folks, it will never be good enough for some and they will talk bad about you. I meet many people who forsake the Word of God in order to be socially accepted and have good things said about them by those in their circle. That may be fine for your circle, but what is God saying about us? The Bible says this in John 1:47: "As they approached, Jesus said, 'Now here is a genuine son of Israel—a man of complete integrity.'"

What Jesus had to say about Nathanael is powerful. It prompts me to ask myself, "What is God saying about me?" Won't you join me in asking, "What is God saying about us?" Prayerfully, like Nathanael, He says we have integrity, dedication to Him. We are true to the faith and are a part of the chosen church—the church of Philadelphia. We may take what God says about us for granted now, but that will change when we stand before Him to be judged. Allow God the opportunity to say good things about you. I will do the same in Jesus's name.

God bless you!

Not a Child Anymore

Everyone has a little bit of childish behavior left in them. Maybe we have a tantrum when we don't get something we desire, or, perhaps, we're needy as a newborn. Me? I'd say it's my love for Frosted Flakes, even wanting to replace my dinner with them. While these are seemingly small matters, as a child grows and developmental progress is not where it's supposed to be, it's cause for concern. For example, a twelve-year-old wetting the bed every night would be an area of concern. What about the spiritual child? When we accept Christ, we are as newborns in our faith. Should two years pass and we're committing the same ungodly acts, it's also an area of concern.

The Apostle Paul says this in 1 Corinthians 13:11: "When I was a child, I spoke and thought and reasoned as a child. But when I grew up, I put away childish things." What is it we need to put away as proof that we no longer are babes in the Lord? Is it lying? Gossip? Unforgiveness? The best way to show that we have grown is to exercise the love of Christ to all men.

Grow up today. and rid yourself of those areas our Heavenly Father has to be concerned with.

God bless you!

It's About Faith...It's About Trust

It is simply amazing how people will put their faith and trust in people, places, and things but ignore God. Let us not forget that we serve a miracle-working God through His Son, Jesus Christ. Two blind men wanted to see, and, yes, you guessed it—they put their faith in Jesus for healing. See with me what happened in Matthew 9:28–30. It reads: "They went right into the house where he was staying, and Jesus asked them, 'Do you believe I can make you see?' 'Yes, Lord,' they told Him, 'we do.' Then He touched their eyes and said, 'Because of your faith, it will happen.' Then their eyes were opened, and they could see!" That's what I'm talking about.

The same is true today, but we need to turn our doubt into trust and our fear into faith. Jesus Christ is the same yesterday, today, and forever (Hebrews 13:8). We are the ones who change, but He stays the same. He is more than able to grant our heart's desire based on our level of faith in Him. Let us truly begin to trust God by faith in Jesus Christ and prove it by our actions. Faith without works is dead. Let's live out what we confess and become good examples for others to follow. God will bless you because of your faith.

God bless you!

Ministry and Business

Finding a balance between ministry and business can be difficult for the person in survival mode. While tough, we still need to address the areas in our lives that need attention where ministry is concerned. Yes, we have to support our families, but we cannot ignore our calling. For example, the Apostle Paul worked but still did ministry.

The Bible says this in Acts 18:3–4: Paul lived and worked with them, for they were tentmakers just as he was. Each Sabbath found Paul at the synagogue, trying to convince Jews and Greeks alike." In addition to tent making, Paul still did what God called him to do. What about you, Christian? Are you so busy about your business that you have no time for God's business? May I suggest you start your ministry of sharing the Good News before God permanently relieves you of it?

Jesus mandates every believer to tell this Good News to everyone everywhere (Mark 16:15.) We all have a ministry. It's time to go out and evangelize. Send e-mail or text messages, or hold a sign on the corner. Do something to get the word out that Jesus Christ is Lord, He died for us, He loves us, and He is coming soon. Ask yourself: what's more important—my business or God's business? I pray you make the right choice.

God bless you!

Surviving the Hunger Games

Are you hungry right now? If the answer is yes, then I am quite sure you've already planned on a favorite dish that will defeat your hunger. If you are fasting, that's different. Mankind seeks to satisfy a need without giving it a second thought. Talk about needs—are you aware that there are many people in church today who are not part of the Kingdom of God? They are not totally sold out for God; hence, they are spiritually hungry—or *starving* is more like it.

Why not turn to Jesus and be fed today? John 6:35 says this: "Jesus replied, 'I am the bread of life. Whosoever comes to me will never be hungry again. Whoever believes in me will never be thirsty.'" For those who know they aren't saved, you too can survive the hunger games by taking a step of faith to Jesus. The Spirit of God has revealed that when an individual attends a Bible-teaching church service but then leaves without accepting Christ, it is the same as feeling really hungry, going to an all-you-can-eat buffet but then leave hungry because you've decided not to eat. Feed your spirit, man. We must survive to stay alive so that we can arrive in the Kingdom.

God bless you!

Though We May Suffer, People of God Live Forever

Every day I hear about a new form of attack Christians are facing. This lets me know that we are so close to seeing Jesus Christ face-to-face. We don't like suffering in any way. Unfortunately, we live in a fallen world, and it's part of the "walking with God" package. The good news? Our end will be spectacular when we live forever in glory with our King. The Bible says this in 1 Peter 4:12–13: "Dear friends, don't be surprised at the fiery trials you are going through, as if something strange were happening to you. Instead, be very glad—for these trials make you partners with Christ in His suffering, so that you will have the wonderful joy of seeing His glory when it is revealed to all the world."

So, count it all joy, my friends. Be glad, for this is temporary. Look at it like a vacation spot that wasn't what you expected. Make the best of it while looking forward to going home. Heaven is the true home for the follower of Christ. Don't stress the mess here on earth. Where we are going is free from suffering. However, for the unsaved, they will go to the most severe place of suffering. Think about it and choose eternal life.

God bless you!

Holy? Are You Sure?

Instructions in the Word of God are so clear it amazes me. Our Heavenly Father really knows us better than we know ourselves.

A first-time car buyer should consult the operator's manual for instructions. The same is true for a new believer. He or she should consult the manual for specific instructions. One very important instruction states that as Christians, we must be holy. The Bible reference is 1 Peter 1:15–16: "But now you must be holy in everything you do, just as God who chose you is holy. For the scriptures say, "You must be holy because I am holy."

Here's a secret: we cannot be holy without the Holy Spirit. We can put on a good show and receive an Academy Award but without the Holy Spirit, we are not holy. Holy people still sin, yes, but we don't practice sin. Holy people will not act on premeditated sin and then say, "It's no big deal." The Holy Spirit does not lie, so holy people speak the truth. Satan is the father of lies. Please don't utilize his attributes. We must be holy in order to be like God and to live with God for all eternity. It is of great importance. My advice? Make holiness your priority. Ask God to reveal and remove all affiliation with anything unholy. Become holy. The Holy Spirit Himself will appreciate it.

God bless you!

Build Others Up, Don't Tear Them Down

I often hear Christians belittling others, name-calling, gossiping about folks with other believers, or even nonbelievers, and highlighting others' shortcomings. We are to make room for others' faults (Ephesians 4:2) so that our love will be evident. When we truly love God, we lose the appetite we may have once had for putting someone down. Our new spirit instructs us to build others up, so we shouldn't go against Him.

This is what the Bible says in Romans 15:1–2: "We who are strong must be considerate of those who are sensitive about things like this. We must not just please ourselves. We should help others do what is right and build them up in the Lord." Let's start building up today everyone you come in contact with in Jesus's name. God through His grace forgave us and gave us hope. Something powerful I heard: "Mankind gets and forgets, but God gives and forgives!" Become a giver just as our Heavenly Father and show the light of Christ to others. The world is already full of folks who tear down. Live differently starting today. Stretch yourself even further. Apologize to those you've already put down and begin to build them up. It will do wonders for your friendship and for your calling to love. Go ahead, start today!

God bless you!

Mouthwash or Clorox?

Is it me, or has the world become more accepting of foul language? I've even encountered those who justify their filthy language or defend it. Yes, we all know it's a free country and we have freedom of speech; however, we must choose wisely. Let me explain. Each time someone curses, they actually curse themselves. No sin goes unpunished. Don't use simple vocabulary to invite punishment. The Bible says this in Ephesians 4:29: "Don't use foul or abusive language. Let everything you say be good and helpful, so that your words will be an encouragement to those who hear them."

Here we are given specific instructions regarding communication. Now, for the filthy mouth individual, my question: what will it be—mouthwash or clorox? Allow God to change you now. It's an easier, less painful process, like rinsing with mouthwash. But delay in continuous hardheadedness may lead you to a clorox cleansing. Turn to God today. Accept Jesus Christ as Lord and Savior and watch your life change for the better. Your speech will change because your heart has changed. Call on Jesus. He will answer you and cleanse you.

God bless you!

Our Actions Will Show Them Our Father

"Show me your friends, and I will tell you who you are!" While this may be true, I believe a more powerful statement would be, "Our actions will show them our Father."

In John 8:44, Jesus accused the Pharisees of being sons of the devil, who is the father of lies. So, on many occasions, Jesus addressed the people by saying, "I tell you the truth." Even His own disciples were not clear about who He was, so he had to spell it out for them in John 14:10–11: "Don't you believe that I am in the Father and the Father is in me? The words I speak are not my own, but my Father who lives in me does His work through me. Just believe that I am in the Father and the Father is in me. Or at least believe because of the work you have seen me do."

Actions do speak louder than words. Allow others to see God as our Father. The choice is ours to make daily. Don't give a few days to God and the rest to the devil. Mankind may be fooled by our actions, but we can't fool God. Let's get real in our faith. Show the world who your Father is. If you are ashamed to live the Gospel, you can't live with the Father in Heaven. However, you will live with your true Father, Satan. Think about it.

God bless you!

Not the Library but the Sanctuary

I remember getting my library card as a youngster. It gave me access to a wealth of information that would take many lifetimes to read through it all. The library is a great place to spend time, but the sanctuary is far better. In his day, Asaph had issues with wicked folks prospering, so much so that he questioned his faith in God. He did not get a satisfactory answer from friends, the newspaper, or the library; he got it only from the sanctuary. The Bible says this in Psalm 73:16–18: "So I tried to understand why the wicked prosper. But what a difficult task it is! Then I went into your sanctuary, O God, and I finally understood the destiny of the wicked. Truly, you have put them on a slippery path and send them sliding over the cliff to destruction."

Let's face the facts: if we attend a Bible-teaching church, the Word of God should answer our life's questions. Life can be frustrating at various times, but we serve a God who will supply all our needs according to His riches in glory. Don't sit and worry over things you can't change. Go to the house of God and pray for change. When the corporate anointing is present, you can expect a miracle. Go to church and give God your heart. He is able to care for it in a way that we cannot.

God bless you!

Honoring God

Some folks believe that honoring God is not of great importance because we are under grace. Don't confuse grace with a lifestyle of disgrace. For instance, when we are tempted to lie, yet we speak the truth, we honor God by speaking the truth. Perhaps, this misunderstanding is caused by lack of knowledge. Well, here is some knowledge. We honor God by keeping His Word. We should honor Him for being the Word.

The Bible says this in Psalm 29:1–2: "Honor the Lord, you heavenly beings, honor the Lord for his glory and strength. Honor the Lord for the glory of His name. Worship the Lord in the splendor of His holiness." My friends: it may seem like a tall order, but with God, all things are possible. It all comes down to the choices we make. Are they holy or unholy? Yes, we make mistakes, but are we purposely making them while reassuring ourselves that "God knows I'm only human"? Let's get real in our honoring of God, for only He truly deserves honor. We honor our husbands, wives, children, parents, bosses, animals, even our vehicles. How about honoring the true and living God? Start today. It's food for thought, especially since we know we serve a jealous God. Let's honor God in our walk and our talk. So what if we've sinned in the past? Ask God's forgiveness and try your best to let that sin be your last. Honor God, and He will honor you.

God bless you!

Value Menu

In an effort to attract customers, many fast food restaurants have added a value menu. Great, right? Who doesn't desire more for their money? However, many believers have implemented their own spiritual value menu. This is not approved by God. You know, the truth, but not the whole truth; just the appetizer without the main course.

The Bible says this in Hebrews 2:1: "So we must listen very carefully to the truth we have heard, or we may drift away from it." Many who were once close to God the Father and the Lord Jesus Christ have drifted away from the truth. Good, authentic fellowship with the Lord has been reduced to an occasional prayer and/or minimal Bible reading. Do not allow Satan's negative influence to cause you to develop a spiritual value menu. Cling to the truth, who is Jesus. Rekindle your desire to know Him and not just know *of* Him. Don't just attend church; *be* the church, the bride of Christ. Dining with Jesus is the real deal, the original Happy Meal. The value menu subtracts from the norm. Don't jeopardize your spirit, man! Enjoy a rich relationship with your Maker. Rather than reach for the spiritual value meal, treat yourself to the Supersize.

God bless you!

Better Than Frosted Flakes

If you were to ask what my favorite cereal is, Kellogg's Frosted Flakes comes to mind. In its TV commercial, Tony the Tiger, who's on the cereal box, shouts, "They'rrrre great!" *Great* is a strong description that we often assign to individuals who've accomplished extraordinary things. When I hear the word *great*, my Lord comes to mind because he is the ultimate great one.

The Bible says this in Psalm 40:16: "But may all who search for you be filled with joy and gladness in you. May those who love your salvation repeatedly shout, 'The Lord is great!'"

We who love the Lord should proclaim his greatness to the world at large. There are many who seldom think of the Lord due to their "busy schedules." When we testify that the Lord is great, we have them thinking about God, even if for a few seconds. That is seed planting, my friend. Let's have folks wondering why we're full of peace and joy, and when they ask, say the Lord is great, even better than Frosted Flakes. Proclaim His greatness today and every day because that is what He calls us to do.

God bless you!

Faith to Overcome

There are many stories of victory in the Bible. One of my favorites is when Abraham rescued Lot from captivity. It really took some faith to overcome a king and his subjects who just walked over the kings of Sodom and Gomorrah. Without further ado, this is what the Bible says in Genesis 14:14–16: "When Abram heard that his nephew Lot had been captured, he mobilized the 318 trained men who had been born into his household. Then he pursued Kedorlaomer's army until he caught up with them at Dan. Abram recovered all the goods that had been taken, and he brought back his nephew Lot with his possessions and all the women and other captives."

This story inspires me to exercise my faith and take back what the devil stole from me. We can go on complaining about things with no results, or we can use faith to overcome. What are your challenges today? Finances? Has the devil stolen your child to drug addition or your spouse to verbal or physical abuse? Get your trained angels fired up and ready for war through your faithful prayers. It is simple—if we have the faith to overcome, we will overcome because we are more than conquerors in Christ Jesus. Live out your faith.

God bless you!

What Do You Claim?

"I am a Christian," Jim says to his buddy, Tom, who's just caught him in the act of telling a lie. Tom responds, "I'm glad I don't attend your church!"

Please be advised that true worshippers worship God in spirit and in truth. A lying tongue is an abomination to the Lord. If we claim to follow God, let's leave the evil behind and go forward with righteousness.

This is what the Bible says in 2 Timothy 2:19: "But God's truth stands firm like a foundation stone with this inscription: 'The Lord knows those who are his,' and 'Those who claim they belong to the Lord must turn away from all wickedness.'"

What do you claim? If you're hiding your secret sin, then you are claiming that you belong to Satan. The best way to turn from sin is to confront it and recognize it for what it is. We can then repent of our sin, and God will help us on the straight and narrow road. Let's turn away from all wickedness and boldly claim that we follow the Lord. For all eternity, I will be with my Jesus. Option B? For all eternity, be separated from Jesus. What's your claim? For me, Option A will do just fine. Claim life, my friends.

God bless you!

The Rapture After Raptures

Talk about the rapture is not so popular anymore. A few still talk about it, but most are more concerned about life here on earth. The Bible speaks about raptures that occurred in the past, such as Enoch's in Genesis 5:24, Elijah's in 2 Kings 2:11, and Jesus's in Acts 1:9. These have already taken place and been confirmed by witnesses. Where does that leave us? I am glad you asked.

The rapture is the next major biblical event to happen. According to events worldwide, the stage has already been set. This is how the Bible says it will happen in 1 Corinthians 15:52: It will happen in a moment, in the blink of an eye. When the last trumpet sounds, those who have died will be raised to live forever, and we who are living will be transformed, "for our dying bodies must be transformed into bodies that will never die." Is this real or make believe? Let me lovingly say this: you don't want to be left behind to be subjected to the Antichrist's tricks and deception. Start looking into your eternity now. Decide if you want to be a part or not. If you want to be a part of God's family, conduct yourself like royalty and leave the filthy lifestyle alone. Only then will you know for sure that you are ready for the rapture. See you there.

God bless you!

The Bodybuilder

I remember the days when I would go to the gym at least four times a week to work on my body. As selfish as I was, I didn't know it. Bodybuilding isn't bad; it's just that building the body of Christ is better.

The Bible says this in 1 Timothy 4:8: "Physical training is good, but training for godliness is much better, promising benefits in this life and in the life to come."

Placing a system of value on everything you do will help you decide what to do daily. Studying, speaking, and living the Word of God is a really good bodybuilder. Let's invest our time in building up our bodies to the glory of God. We shouldn't neglect physical training of our bodies. But don't over do it. Study to show yourself approved by God, and then your spiritual body will be in shape. Share what you learn and build others up spiritually.

Be the bodybuilder that God calls us to be. Work it out.

God bless you!

The Ultimate Power Position

People are attracted to power. What signifies power? Money, title, position…Many CEOs control the livelihood of their staff and their families. As powerful as that may seem, to be president of the United States is a more recognizable power position because he commands the military. Does it stop there? Absolutely not. The ultimate power position belongs to Jesus. Jesus says this when addressing the council of priests in Matthew 26:64: "And in the future you will see the Son of Man seated in the place of power at God's right hand and coming on the clouds of heaven."

It doesn't get any better than that, my friends. So, just how powerful are the true people of God? Very powerful! We have the DNA of Jesus flowing through our spirit. It is time for believers to start believing and stop being powerless when confronted by the devil. We have the ultimate power in us. Let's start living that way and be victorious over sin. God so loved us that He gave us His Son. The Son gave up His life for us and then gave us His Spirit, which represents power over evil. Trust God with all your heart and use the power of the Holy Spirit to your benefit.

God bless you!

You Are Being Video-Taped!

Many people get excited to learn that a video production is in progress—a music video, church play, even a home birthday party. Whatever the occasion, we put our best foot forward for that video in the way that we dress, act, etc. The reason is that, good or bad, we know someone will see the video. Here's something to think about: we are being video-taped every single minute of every day by God. How well do we dress for the occasion? How have we conducted ourselves for the recording?

The Bible says this in Revelation 20:12: "I saw the dead, both great and small, standing before God's throne. And the books were opened, including the Book of Life. And the dead were judged according to what they had done, as recorded in the books." The awesome thing about God's video tape is that He never loses any footage. For the repentant soul, He will not hold our sins against us because we now live for Jesus Christ. But for the unrepentant, well, the viewing won't be pretty. So, remember: each day you are being video-taped, so conduct yourselves accordingly. Give God, our Father, and the Lord Jesus Christ something great to watch. At the same time, you'll make the devil mad. The video tape of life has no cut and splice, only "Action!"

God bless you!

None Can Compare

In this world, there are many gods worshipped unknowingly by individuals. Those gods vary—money, cars, houses, boyfriends, girlfriends, and the like. In the grand scheme of things, we still have the true God who is ruler of all. To Him, there is no comparison. The Bible tells us this in Isaiah 46:4–5: "I will be your God throughout your lifetime until your hair is white with age. I made you, and will care for you. I will carry you along and save you. To Whom will you compare me? Who is my equal?"

The answer to both questions: no one. No one cares for us like our Heavenly Father. His mercies are new every morning. He does not allot the full punishment for our sins. How great is our God and greatly to be praised. Rid yourselves of any and every god you might have in your heart where your creator ought to be. For those of you who might think you don't need God, well, you worship the god of self in your heart.

Ask yourself this: can you compete with Jesus? The answer is No. Neither you or anyone else can compare. Give God the glory due Him through his Son, Jesus Christ. Don't waste any more time wandering in the wilderness. No romance or finance can compare with our God. Won't you surrender to Him today?

God bless you!

He Did No Wrong

If you are human, you are prone to doing something wrong. We make mistakes and sometimes don't even know it. Our Heavenly Father saw our fallen state and decided to send Jesus to reinstate us back to Himself. What was the requirement? Jesus had to remain sin-free from birth through Mary all the way to Calvary where He would die for you and me. It was the only way He could pay the price for our sin.

Did He do anything wrong? He absolutely did not. As a matter of fact, even before He was born, this is what the Bible says in Isaiah 53:9: "He had done no wrong and had never deceived anyone. But He was buried like a criminal; He was put in a rich man's grave." No one else in history has a perfect record but Jesus. Please keep in mind He was born to be a light for a season, but His main purpose was to die for our sins. A sacrificial Savior, a friend, a Messiah, Jesus is His name!

Do you really love and trust Him today? We know how much we love Him by the amount of wrong we continue to do or refuse to do. Allow His conviction to make you more like Him. After all, that's what Christianity is all about. Let's do right!

God bless you!

He Came to Make Us Rich

This kind of topic grabs attention. People everywhere want to know how they can become rich. The question is what kind of riches am I talking about? Are they riches that are here today, gone tomorrow? Or are they riches that will last an eternity?

The Bible says this in 2 Corinthians 8:9: "You know the generous grace of our Lord Jesus Christ. Though He was rich, yet for your sakes He became poor, so that by His poverty He could make you rich." Jesus wants us to be rich in spirit. When the Holy Spirit leads and guides us in all righteousness, then we are truly wealthy. People who have monetary riches without Jesus are normally miserable and lack peace. On the other hand, when God grants monetary riches to the true believer, He adds no stress or sorrow to it.

Become rich in the Spirit of Christ; after all, that is why He came. To open your account, repent of your sins and invite Jesus in. Then, everything you do for His glory—from saying, "Praise the Lord," to "God bless you"—your account will be credited. Start your journey on becoming a spiritual billionaire today.

God bless you!

Will You Rise or Will You Fall?

Many times I've heard people say they have friends who are in the same position they were in ten years ago. I too am guilty of such a statement, but let me say this: we were wrong. After a deep study of God's Word, I realize people change daily. Perhaps, financially some stay the same but not spiritually.

Let's say, for instance, you have a friend who began attending church and received salvation but his or her financial breakthrough has yet to arrive. You may misjudge that individual. You may conclude that they must be in a fallen state when in fact they are on the rise. The Bible says this in Psalm 75:7: "It is God alone who judges; He decides who will rise and who will fall."

The cover of your story may read, "on the rise," but what do your inner pages say? God is searching for true worshippers who'll rise up and be a witness this season. Remember: stagnant water stinks. Rise up and do more for God. At bare minimum, talk to one person about Jesus daily. What constitutes a fall? It's drifting away from God and making our business more important than His business. Get it straight before it's too late. Rise, my friend, and don't fall. Rise, my friend!

God bless you!

A Peaceful Little

Many financially poor individuals desire to be financially rich, but ironically many financially rich individuals desire to be rich in peace.

Why is that? You see, true peace cannot be purchased with financial wealth. Only with spiritual wealth can one attain peace. After having chased money for many years, people tell me that if they could go back in time and do things differently, they definitely would. They believe that the spiritual sacrifices they made in order to climb the corporate ladder left an empty feeling in their hearts.

The Bible says this in Proverbs 15:16: "Better to have little, with fear for the Lord, than to have great treasure and inner turmoil." Now, I'm not an advocate for remaining poor. I'm simply saying that one should consider the cost before ignoring God only to work every day in order to accumulate money. Establish a personal relationship with God and watch Him grant you peace like a river flowing. If you allow finances to remove the peace you once shared with God, just remember: you cannot bring finances into the next life. It's better to have a peaceful little with contentment. You know I am right. Seek God today. Confess your sin and begin to truly enjoy the Prince of Peace.

God bless you!

The Real Checklist

In preparation for vacation, we usually pack a bag. The truly organized individual may use a checklist to ensure basic necessities aren't left behind. I love the fact that we can use this simple concept in getting ready for our trip to heaven.

Packing clothes and a toothbrush are necessary for earthly travel, but what about packing for heaven? Micah 6:8 shares a checklist that we should all abide by: "No, O people, the Lord has told you what is good, and this is what He requires of you: to do what is right, to love mercy, and to walk humbly with your God."

In other words, we know what is right, so choose to do it instead of doing wrong. Be merciful and forgiving to others. Then, walk humbly with God. Pray His will be done in your life daily and then submit to His will. This checklist will get you to heaven, my friend; however, it is impossible to do without the Holy Spirit helping you. Repeat after me: Lord God, I repent of my sins. Wash me clean and make me new. Thank you, Jesus, for dying on the cross for me. Come into my heart and stay with me forever. In Jesus's name, I pray. Amen.

Congratulations! You can check number one off of your checklist. Continue with the rest as you humbly walk with God.

God bless you!

Got Milk?

A question for you spiritual minds out there: how many catastrophes will God allow an individual, a family, or a nation just to keep His Word? Let's take a look at Joshua 5:6. "The Israelites had traveled in the wilderness for forty years until all the men who were old enough to fight in battle when they left Egypt had died. For they had disobeyed the Lord, and the Lord vowed he would not let them enter the land he had sworn to give us—a land flowing with milk and honey."

It's scary to imagine that disobeying God will cause us to miss out on major blessings, or even kill us. My advice: write down all known acts of disobedience in your life and prayerfully ask God to remove them. I know some won't do it because they place a lower value on eternity, but what about this life? You may still access your land of milk and honey by repenting of your sins and turning to God the Father and our Lord Jesus Christ. You will find peace and rest for your souls. Get started today and have your dairy. For those who are lactose intolerant, have some honey. Don't make excuses. Make good use of the time allotted to you to change.

God bless you!

The Overflow of Blessings

Everyone loves a blessing. It sure beats a curse, but be careful. Sometimes we receive a curse and mistake it for a blessing. For instance, we get a new job with hours above our normal forty-hour week. The job now subtracts from family, church, and even personal devotion time. So is it really a blessing or a curse? Well, the answer will lie with each individual. The anointed of God will sense quality time with God and family as a major part of their lives missing. For those whose God is money, it will be no big deal.

Keep in mind what David, God's anointed one, said in Psalm 23:5: "You prepare a feast for me in the presence of my enemies. You honor me by anointing my head with oil. My cup overflows with blessings." All believers have access to blessings that will overflow. The secret: you must have a heart after God. God grants us the same opportunities. He did it for David, and He will overflow your cup as well. He will reward those who diligently seek Him. Get off the sidelines. Quit complaining. Change your lifestyle to one that truly glorifies God and see what He does for you. It's time you get a bigger cup and watch God cause it to overflow. I dare you to trust Him.

God bless you!

Here Comes the Victory

Running a marathon takes more than just physical ability. It also takes having the right mindset. While running, you patiently wait to cross the finish line. The same is true on our Christian journey. We keep running expecting the victory as we wait on the Lord for the rapture or to cross over into eternity.

The Bible says this in Psalm 62:1–2: "I wait quietly before God, for my victory comes from Him. He alone is my rock and my salvation, my fortress where I will never be shaken." Our victories come in many ways, so expect them—physical victory over sickness, emotional victory over heartbreak, financial victory over lack, and, most importantly, spiritual victory over the devil.

My friends, it is time to walk and talk as children of the King. We are fighting a fixed war; the victory is already ours. Don't allow battle scars to discourage you from continuing to fight. Apply your bandages and keep on fighting. Even if you weep all night, just remember that victorious joy will come in the morning. If you expect it, you will get it. If you don't, then you won't.

God bless you!

Don't Wait until You're Out of Gas

It's a terrible thing to be on the highway, miles away from an exit, and run out of gas. I know things happen, but some things can be prevented. A few years ago, a woman ran out of gas, and then a stranger seemingly stopping to help robbed and killed her. You may think that to be extreme, but what about running out of gas spiritually? If we as believers monitored our spiritual gas tanks the way we do our car's, the backslide rate would be less than one percent. We look at our gas tanks, know where it can take us, and fill up if it is insufficient.

The Bible says this in Proverbs 14:8: "The prudent understand where they are going, but fools deceive themselves." Don't be self-deceiving. If your Spirit man is running low on fuel, refill before you're empty. We encounter many backsliders along the spiritual highway hanging out with nonbelievers. Let me lovingly say this: Satan has a plan for everyone in such a position, and that plan includes eternal separation from God. My advice to those who care to change is simply this: pray to God and repent through His Son, Jesus Christ. Ask Him to fill your "tank" with Himself—the Holy Spirit—and then make regular visits to the spiritual gas station—a good bible-teaching church, that is. Don't run out of fuel.

God bless you!

Can't Buy Your Way Out

We've heard it at least once before—someone beating their case having been able to afford the right priced attorney. Some individuals then commit more crimes knowing they can buy their way out. While money can buy protection, witnesses, and so on, that type of mindset is very foolish. There will come a day when we all must face Jesus Christ, the righteous judge, and money cannot help anyone on that day.

As a matter of fact, the Bible says this in Proverbs 11:4: "Riches won't help on the day of judgment, but right living can save you from death." Death in this area of scripture means eternal separation from God—the second death. Pay close attention to how you value money. Place a higher value on your relationship with God. Test yourself: when you wake up in the morning, do you first think of God and desire to spend time with Him in prayer or devotion? Or do you first think of your job and making money? Make a change. Pray and ask God to solve your problems rather than run to your money. Trust in the Lord more than money, and He will make a way for you now and on the day of judgment. You can't bribe God.

God bless you!

Multiply Your Days

Imagine the billboard AD on the highway: "Lessen your days on earth! Partake in this activity!" How may people do you think would quickly respond? Not many, right? I'll let you in on a secret. Many billboard ads do say just that, but it takes wisdom in order to understand.

Many people lack wisdom because they don't live for God. True wisdom only comes from God, not those Ivy League schools but from a really close and personal relationship with God. When we possess true wisdom, this is what we can expect: Proverbs 9:11: "Wisdom will multiply your days and add years to your life." That is powerful! Don't take this lightly, my friend. If you do, your life might just come to an early end. Seek God with your whole heart and not just for what he can do for you. Get to know Him as a cool, all-knowing friend. We spend so much time talking to non-progressive friends who sometimes endanger our lives. Let's stop being foolish and seek the wisdom that will multiply our days. Then we'll be able to see subtle, demonic messages on billboards about gambling, engaging in sexual sin, etc., and we can begin to pray for the eyes of others to be opened! Today you can start multiplying your days.

God bless you!

Today and Beyond

Thinking about the past can be sad, or it can be glad depending on what it is we remember. I sometimes remember the ways in which Satan tricked me into sin or played guilt trip games on me. Nowadays, I try my very best to keep my focus not just on today but in preparation for eternity. We, as Christians, should all have this mindset not only for ourselves but also to inspire others. The Bible says this in Hebrews 3:13–14: "You must warn each other every day, while it is still today, so that none of you will be deceived by sin and hardened against God. For if we are faithful to the end, trusting God just as firmly as when we first believed, we will share in all that belongs to Christ."

Don't worry about tomorrow for today has enough trouble of its own. However, we should plan for tomorrow in order to be that vessel God can use for His glory. Our lives are no longer our own if we belong to Christ Jesus, so let's put a bigger emphasis on eternity with God. Try and encourage as many people as we can to see what we see. Start thinking today and beyond and of the gracious favor we enjoy having received salvation. If you have not received His salvation, give your life to Jesus today and begin laboring for the Lord. Your reward will continue for all eternity.

God bless you!

Start with a Good Foundation

All around, we hear talks of prosperity, wealth building, and future secure lifestyles. There's nothing wrong with that because if we fail to plan, that means we plan to fail. Nonetheless, don't get consumed with your desires before setting a good foundation in Jesus Christ who is the solid rock. Jesus tells us this in Matthew 7:26–27: "But anyone who hears my teaching and doesn't obey it is foolish, like a person who builds a house on sand. When the rains and floods come and the winds beat against that house, it will collapse with a mighty crash."

It is so easy to read the Word of God or hear him from a teacher and then not obey. You may even convince yourself that God understands that you are only human, and you can't do any better. That frame of mind and sinful lifestyle is called foolish or foods in action. Don't waste your time overworking on earthly wealth or partying hard and forsake your everlasting dwelling with God. You don't want to spend so much time building on a sand-like foundation. Pray daily to God the Father in the name of Jesus and ask Him to show you His will and give you the strength to do it. When you truly desire to please Him, I guarantee He will be pleasing to you. Expect the rewards that are attached to truly serving the Lord.

God bless you!

Don't Forget Whom We Serve

Oftentimes, we forget whom we serve. We focus on the seemingly impossible in life instead of what is possible with God. The Bible tells us in Genesis 18 that Sarah doubted when God said she would have a baby in her old age. She thought that would be too hard to do. However, this is the Lord's reply in verse 14: "Is anything too hard for the Lord? I will return about this time next year, and Sarah will have a son."

Maybe your doubts and flaws are a little different from Sarah's; she had good finances, a good husband, handmaids, among others. Maybe you're the opposite today, you have children but no husband or wife, maybe your finances are a mess, or you have an illness. Don't forget whom we serve. The same God who did it for Sarah will do it for you and me. Our job is to believe His Word and praise Him with our lifestyle. Love the Lord with all you've got, and He will give unto you your heart's desires. There is no problem or situation that our great God cannot rectify and satisfy. Begin to truly trust Him, my friends, not only with lip service but also in the way you think, talk, and live, and He will come through for you.

God bless you!

To Whom Do You Bring Joy?

Our actions can bring joy to some and sadness to others. Since we can all agree to that, let's narrow it down to two individuals: God the Father and Satan. Jesus chose to bring joy to His Father, therefore, it was sadness to Satan.

The Bible tells us this in Mark 1:11: "And a voice from Heaven said, 'You are my dearly loved Son, and you bring me great joy.'" How about you today, friend? Do you consider your actions before you do them, making sure they'll bring joy to God? Remember, if our actions don't bring joy to God, they bring joy to our enemy, Satan.

Let me encourage you today to pay close attention to what you do, say, and think about daily. Making Satan joyful will result in eternal punishment. On the other hand, to make God joyful will bring an eternal reward. Analyze before you exercise and you will be wise. The enemy is very tricky, but we have access to the Holy Spirit in order to counteract his tricks and put him under our feet. Make God smile all the while, and He will be more than glad to reciprocate.

God bless you!

Fortune-Telling in the Churches

A famous line from one psychic's advertisement was, "Call me now!" Since people naturally like to hear good things that will happen for them, some call upon a psychic, unaware that the psychic or fortune-teller is there to do just that: tell you a fortune. They accomplish this by listening to your problems and then telling you what they think you want to hear.

The Bible says this in Leviticus 19:26: "Do not practice fortune telling or witchcraft." Sadly enough, some pastors don't read this area of scripture, and they tell the people what they want to hear in the name of prophecy. Be careful! Stop fortune-telling just to make a fortune. A true prophet drives fear in the heart of the people as Samuel did with the Israelites. When the man of God arrived, he was asked whether he'd come in peace or to rebuke.

If you're attending church for the future-telling, then it's time to repent and get on the right path. I know of people who go to church, sit close to the prophet or prophetess, hoping they're called out about a new job, a new home, a raise in pay if they'd only sow a seed, and so on and so forth. My advice to you: simply read your Bible and decipher true prophecy from fortune-telling. Don't get mad with me. Be glad for the truth.

God bless you!

100 Percent

Why is 100 percent so important? Well, here are a few thoughts: what if on your way to work your car only worked 50 percent of the time? Chances are you would soon be unemployed. What if your flight only went 95 percent of your destination? You would still need to arrange for additional travel. The point is this, my friend: we should not neglect 100 percent when dealing with God's Word. Don't just read what makes you feel cushy and blessed. What about reproof and dealing with sin?

The Bible says this in 2 Timothy 3:16–17: "All scripture is inspired by God and is useful to teach us what is true and to make us realize what is wrong in our lives. It corrects us when we are wrong and teaches us to do what is right. God uses it to prepare and equip His people to do every good work." Giving 100 percent means the same as all, so we can say 100 percent of scripture is inspired by God. Let's use the Word of God to our benefit; but before we can, we need to read it in its entirety. The more you read, the more of the Holy Spirit's wisdom you will receive. Living the saved life is a little bit of heaven on earth because of the Holy Spirit Himself. Stay on the right path reading 100 percent and in the future you will enjoy 100 percent of heaven.

God bless you!

The Ultimate Airborne Experience

Flying high above the clouds reminds me of the power of God who gave mankind the ability to make airplanes. Though air travel is fun in most cases, it is not the ultimate airborne experience.

The Bible tells us this in 1 Corinthians 15:52: "For when the trumpet sounds, those who have died will be raised to live forever. And we who are living will also be transformed." This is the rapture, my friend. Can you imagine being caught up in the air to be with Jesus and then staying with Him forever? If your mind is not focused on this near-future experience, your standards are not high enough. Some may feel high and mighty with their own private jet; however, a private jet cannot get you to Jesus in the clouds—only a heart sold out to Jesus can.

So, what are you waiting for? Repent of your sins today. Live for God and not just for yourself. Do these things, and prayerfully I will see you in the clouds as part of the ultimate airborne experience with Jesus. Think about it and then do it. No one knows how much time is left on their earthly clock. Be ready.

God bless you!

It's Your Choice to Serve the Lord

The God of this world has one thing going for Him: "Anything goes!" When an individual chooses not to serve the God of Israel, cursing, lying, stealing, hatred, all these things and more occur without conviction. The enemy, Satan, applauds that type of lifestyle; however, serving Him will lead to a tragic end.

The man of God, Joshua, dealt with the Israelites regarding the idols they held in their hearts. He says this in Joshua 24:14–15: "So fear the Lord and serve Him wholeheartedly. Put away forever the idols your ancestors worshipped when they lived beyond the Euphrates River and in Egypt. Serve the Lord alone. But if you refuse to serve the Lord, then choose today whom you will serve. Would you prefer the gods your ancestors served beyond the Euphrates? Or will it be the gods of the Amorites in whose land you now live? But as for me and my family, we will serve the Lord."

The man of God made a choice. How about you today? Do you serve the god of fornication or the Lord? Do you serve the god of greed or the Lord? It's a choice to serve the Lord, my friends. If you look ahead to the eternal benefits, you'll find it's well worth it. Repent and accept Him today. Don't delay. Start serving Him.

God bless you!

It's Not About Balancing the Scale

During conversation with a local religious leader, good deeds were discussed. Many people actually believe that being a good person will qualify them for heaven. The theory is that God will weigh my bad and my good, and if my good outweighs my bad, I am heaven-bound. So, many individuals then try and make the scale of life just a little off balance to keep good deeds weighing more than bad.

Sounds like a good theory until you read the Word of God. The Bible says this in Ephesians 2:9: Salvation is not a reward for the good things we have done, so none of us can boast about it." The Bible also says in Romans 10:9: "If you confess with your mouth that Jesus is Lord and believe in your heart that God raised Him from the dead, you will be saved."

Salvation does not depend on good deeds. It is based on confession and repenting of our sins to the Lord Jesus Christ. Don't be fooled by blind guides who are leading you to a ditch. Turn to Jesus today and throw your scale away. It is not about a balance in life; it's about living for Christ.

God bless you!

Nothing Better Than This Life

So, what's the best life, one might ask? I tell you this: it is more than just lip service for Christ. It is a life sold out to Christ. Jesus says this in Mark 8:35–37: "If you try to hang on to your life, you will lose it. But if you give up your life for my sake and the sake of the Good News, you will save it. And what do you benefit if you gain the whole world but lose your own soul? Is anything worth more than your soul?"

When I think of all the wealth of the world, it's fascinating but not worth losing my soul. To know I am a citizen of heaven on the mission field called earth is the best life. We have the promises in the Word of God that our souls are saved, which entitles us to spend eternity with Jesus. On the contrary, those who don't seize the opportunity to live a Christlike life and die in that state will spend eternity separated from God and the Lord Jesus Christ. The Bible says in Psalm 32:8, "The Lord says, 'I will guide you along the best pathway for your life. I will advise you and watch over you.'" Now ask yourself this question: what is keeping you from surrendering to Christ? Then ask: is it worth more than your soul? Chew on that and then choose Christ. God wants you to live the life.

God bless you!

If You Can't Work It Out,
Then Walk It Out

Confrontations occur daily. We've all had our share. The question is how do we deal with it? Some argue and use hurtful words, while some do hurtful things just to spite the other. This is bad, especially when either individual is a Christian. My advice is this: try and work things out in a peaceful manner, with love being the basis of your conversation and actions. If the other person decides no can do and you see yourself beginning to get really hot, walk away and cool off. It is best to say nothing than to say something that sins against God.

Look at what Jess says in Matthew 25:40: "And the King will say, 'I tell you the truth, when you did it to one of the least of these my brothers and sisters, you were doing it to me!'" Let's be mindful of the things we say and do to Jesus through his people. In a marriage relationship, it is more difficult to walk away from a hot dispute, but we can still choose our words carefully to show Christ and not Satan. Let us be the godly representatives we are called to be so that the people of the world will notice a significant difference between us and them. Remember: when confronted and blasted, let's love them. Maybe, just maybe, we can save them.

God bless you!

Lower Your Temperature

It doesn't take much to raise some folks' temperature. A word, a look, or some negative body language, and they go crazy giving you a piece of their mind. The funny thing is, after getting all bent out of shape, they often realize it was a misunderstanding. We really need to control our temper, be it intentional disrespect or a misunderstanding.

The Bible says this in Proverbs 19:11 and 19: "Sensible people control their temper; they earn respect for overlooking wrongs." Hot-tempered people must pay the penalty. If you rescue them once, you will have to do it again. Isn't that the truth? A man got into a heated conversation with a friend and stabbed that friend with a butter knife. The friend almost died so that man ended up serving fifteen years in prison for attempted murder. Sharing his story, he said, "If I only waited ten seconds to think things through I wouldn't have wasted fifteen years in prison."

Maybe you haven't gone that far yet, although you've thought about it. Remember, 1 John 3:15 says if you hate someone, you are a murderer at heart. A hot temper is the recipe for anger, hatred, and the path to destruction, so lower your temperature. One of the fruits of the spirit is self-control. Please control your temper. It will make God proud and your life better.

God bless you!

It's a Miracle, My Friend

From time to time, we need to reflect on the days of old and remember what God delivered us from. Personally speaking, my being alive today is truly a miracle, but the biggest miracle in my life is being a continuous mouthpiece for the Lord.

The Bible tells this story in Mark 5:18–20: "As Jesus was getting into the boat, the man who had been demon possessed begged to go with Him. But Jesus said, 'No, go home to your family, and tell them everything the Lord has done for you and how merciful he has been.'" So the man started off to visit the Ten Towns of that region and began to proclaim the great things Jesus had done for him, and everyone was amazed at what he told them.

We need to stop focusing so much on materialistic miracles and take a good look at spiritual miracles for a change. Many of us ignore those miracles of testifying that Jesus is Lord, miracles that we've stopped lying, cursing, or cheating on our spouse. It's a miracle, my friend. Let's thank our miracle-working God for the miracles in our lives. Make requests for spiritual miracles and grow closer to your Maker. To appreciate where you are and where you are going, reflect on your past but keep it in the past. You are a miracle, my friend.

God bless you!

We Need to Talk

We've heard the saying before, "No man is an island," yet some people try and live that way. They keep things bottled up for years without sharing it with someone in whom they can trust. If there's an issue we're struggling with, we should seek out a prayer warrior whom we can trust and share with. Be sure to test the spirit of that person by the Holy Spirit in you. When you know that individual is qualified, then you should share just as the Bible encourages us to do in James 5:16. "Confess your sins to each other and pray for each other so that you may be healed. The earnest prayer of a righteous person has great power and produces wonderful results."

Your healing may be just a prayer away. Start by consulting Jesus. He looks down when we don't pray and says, "We need to talk." Jesus will lead us to individuals with understanding hearts whom we're able to confide in. Don't burst like an over-inflated balloon. Let out some hot air. The ears of Jesus and His true followers won't be closed to His people. If you have not accepted Jesus, accept Him today by inviting Him into your heart and then turn from sin. Again, my friend, talk to Him.

God bless you!

Let's Do Better

If your child comes home with a poor report card, don't tell them they're good for nothing. That would be poor parenting. Instead, assure them that they can do better and that you are willing to help. The same is true for that believer continuing to receive Ds and Fs on his spiritual report card. Be encouraged, and let's do better. As Christians, holiness is what we should live in!

The Bible says this in Romans 6:19: "Because of the weakness of your human nature, I am using the illustration of slavery to help you understand all this. Previously, you let yourselves be slaves to impurity and lawlessness, which led ever deeper into sin. Now you must give yourselves to be slaves to righteous living so that you will become holy."

Study to show yourself approved by God. Live what you've learned and receive an A on your spiritual report card. So you've made a mistake; stop being hard on yourself and do better next time. Need help from God in any area? All you have to do is ask Him. Trying to make it in life all on your own is foolish and sets the stage for failure. However, when we invite Jesus Christ in our hearts to lead and guide us, then victory is truly ours. The best way to do better is to follow the lead of our Savior.

God bless you!

To Be Pure, Read More

The Word of God is so awesome. We receive so many benefits when we not only read the Word but also live it. Folks complain about their struggle with sinful ways—lying, cursing, anger, envy, pornography, and the list goes on—but the only remedy I can offer is, "What does the Word of God say?"

The Lord promises to make us pure after receiving His spirit, but we still need to do our part. The cleansing of a human being takes time; it is not done overnight. It is imperative to be in the Word, which is God's promises. The Bible says this in Psalm 12:6: "The Lord's promises are pure, like silver refined in a furnace, purified seven times over."

How does this work? It's very simple. The Word of God is pure. When we read the Word and live it, we become pure. It starts with reading the Word though because you can't do what you don't know. Start today. Don't delay. This world is full of impurities, so don't get entangled with it. Cling to the Word. Remember: only the pure in heart shall see God. To be pure, read more.

God bless you!

Follow the Exit Signs

When traveling on the highway, we need to read the road signs. However, if we read the sign that tells us to exit and we choose to ignore it, we won't reach our specific destination.

The same is true in our Christian walk. God shows us paths in our lives that we need to exit all the time, paths that will cause us to stumble into sin and keep us away from a close walk with Jesus. When we are tempted to sin, we can remember what the Bible says in 1 Corinthians 10:12–13: "If you think you are standing strong, be careful not to fall. The temptations in your life are no different from what others experience. And God is faithful. He will not allow the temptation to be more than you can stand. When you are tempted, he will show you a way out so that you can endure."

What a powerful verse to retain in your memory bank. When God gives an exit, my friend, just take it. Our final destination is heaven, but if we don't follow God's exit signs, we'll end up somewhere other than. Please pay close attention to the exit signs because most roads lead to hell. Follow the exit signs and leave sin behind.

God bless you!

Are You Hungry?

It's common to hear someone say they're hungry, but to say you are hungry and have no means to eat is really a problem. If you are a provider for your family and lose your job, find a replacement as soon as possible. If the job you desire is not available now, find something to provide food and pay the bills temporarily. Don't get so caught up in your dreams that reality is overlooked. By all means, pursue your dreams, but remember, you still have to eat.

The Bible says this in Proverbs 28:19: "A hard worker has plenty of food, but a person who chases fantasies ends up in poverty."

So, are you hungry right now? If so, what are you doing to change that status? It's okay to use less desirable jobs as stepping stones. Let's analyze the matter and see what pleases God. Jesus never begged anyone for anything. Quite the opposite was true. He was a giver to all. Be like Jesus. Help feed the hungry rather than being hungry yourself. Work is available to all who desire to work.

God bless you!

God Will Not Deny Those Who Rely

From time to time, I remember my childhood years, and one particular fond memory was walking with my mom or my dad. A lot of the time, I had no idea where we were going, but because they held my hand, I didn't care. Now I am all grown-up, and I still feel the same way I did as a little boy. The reason is simply this: my Heavenly Father has stretched out His hand to me, and I have taken it. I rely on Him totally, and there is no need to fear. He sees all I need and provides. As a matter of fact, the Bible says this in Psalm 33:18: "But the Lord watches over those who fear Him, those who rely on His unfailing love."

There you have it, my friends. God will not deny those who rely. Let's be real and ask ourselves this question: do I truly trust God and rely on Him? Or is our faith in a husband, a wife, a girlfriend, or a boyfriend? Why not surrender it all to God today through His Son Jesus Christ? Accept His will for your life. I cannot promise you that it will be an easy road because Satan will hate to lose you, but you can make it with God's strength and power. If you've already accepted Him, be encouraged. Great is your reward.

God bless you!

Don't Just Go with Whatever

How many times have you heard the expression, "Just go with the flow"? Beware of that. After all, you are not a river. People sing songs like, "Que Sera, Sera, whatever will be, will be, the future's not ours to see, Que Sera, Sera." I can agree to some degree; the future is not for us to see in its entirety, but as for whatever will be will be?

Let's see what the Bible says in Matthew 7:13–14 (NLT): "You can enter God's Kingdom only through the narrow gate. The highway to hell is broad, and its gate is wide for the many who choose that way. But the gateway to life is very narrow and the road is difficult, and only a few ever find it."

This means we have a choice. We don't have to remain a slave to sin and end up in judgment for all eternity. Whatever we choose will be is more like it. Everyone has two possible destinies: one is life eternally and the other is eternal death. Don't just go with "whatever." Choose this day whom you will serve. Stop watching to see what everyone else is doing. Decide for yourself to choose Jesus and live for Him, or Satan will decide for you and keep you to himself.

God bless you!

Believe and Just Do It

I like Mike's slogan, "Just do it!" As believers, we can learn from it a spiritual lesson with regard to answering the call God gave us. Casting out demonic spirits and rebuking strongholds are just some of the things Jesus did when He physically walked with His disciples.

This is what He told them in John 14:12: "I tell you the truth, anyone who believes in me will do the same works I have done, and even greater works, because I am going to be with the Father." Jesus passed the mantle on to us for great works. Then, why are we slacking off? Many people are unbelieving believers. Allow me to explain. Some believe in God but not that God can or will use them for great works. It's a matter of seeking God's will for your life and being willing to accept it. That's what it boils down to.

Stop saying you can't because you never will with that attitude. Start saying, "I can do all things through Christ who gives me strength!" Watch for directives from the Holy Spirit. Believe you can and just do it. Stop stalling because it only leads to bawling. Don't grieve the Holy Spirit; work with Him.

God bless you!

Thirst Is Not Always Bad

We all get thirsty at times. Our throat gets dry, and we might feel dehydrated. A drink of water solves the problem most of the time. However, another thirst exists but often goes overlooked. It is the thirst of the soul. If we pay no attention to our thirsty soul, we set ourselves up for eternal failure. If we pay attention to our thirsty soul, it guides us to our Lord and Savior, Jesus Christ, who tells us this in Revelation 21:6: "And He also said, 'It is finished! I am the Alpha and the Omega—the Beginning and the End. To all who are thirsty I will give freely from the springs of the water of life.'"

It is amazing to me to know that a thirst for Jesus will quench my thirst forever. Jesus told the woman at the well that if she drank living water, she would never thirst again. What is living water? The Holy Spirit, who is Jesus in the Spirit, is the living water. Eating and drinking His Word and thirsting for Him daily will satisfy better than anything or anyone else in this world. Obey your thirst and quench it with Jesus.

God bless you!

Prepaid Tolls

Many states have toll roads. In Florida and many other states, you can purchase a sun pass or easy pass—a sensor with prepaid money on it used to pay the tolls. What I love about prepaid toll devices is that it allows you to drive without having to stop completely at a toll booth. What a blessing it is to know that God sent His Son, Jesus Christ, to prepay all the tolls on sin's highway. I say "sin's highway" because Romans 3:23–24 says, "We all have sinned and fall short of God's glorious standard. Yet God, with undeserved kindness, declares that we are righteous. He did this through Christ Jesus, when he freed us from the penalty for our sins."

In essence, when we accept the route God laid out for us, we're driving on the righteous highway. The tolls are prepaid on both highways until our time here on earth has expired! The freedom of choice is a bad one for those who choose the wrong way! Confess your sins to God and accept the free gift of salvation through our Lord and Savior, Jesus Christ. Get on the right highway. Let God know that you truly appreciate the prepaid tolls all the way to heaven.

God bless you!

A Direct Blessing from God's Treasure Chest

You'll catch someone's attention easily by mentioning that you want to bless them. Well, the God who created us really wants to bless us. In fact, He's created treasure chests all over the world for that very purpose. They're called churches. Let's take a look at God's promises in a vision to Ezekiel 47:12, which says, "Fruit trees of all kinds will grow along both sides of the river. The leaves of these trees will never turn brown and fall, and there will always be fruit on their branches. There will be a new crop every month, for they are watered by the river flowing from the Temple. The fruit will be for food and the leaves for healing."

Amazing! Can you imagine a life dedicated to God with services to His church that produce monthly food and healing? I can, along with many other believers. When things appear to get a little low, the blessing comes flowing. Have you given your life to Christ? Are you connected with a Bible-teaching church of Jesus Christ? If not, don't blame God for your lack of blessings—peace, joy, financial stability, and a constant glimpse of your home in heaven. That's correct—when the children of God gather to worship, it's a glimpse of heaven. Invest in God's treasure chest. Be the church.

God bless you!

You Decide Your Own Speech

Choices, choices, choices—we make them every day, don't we? Even if we sit at home and do nothing, it's still a choice. I might add, it is extremely important to choose our words carefully. Analyze conversation and decide to speak positive words rather than negative ones. Wandering minds might ask, "Why should I do that?"

My reply is simply this: if you believe in God and His Word, hear His reasoning from Matthew 12:36–37: "And I tell you this, you must give an account on judgment day for every idle word you speak. The words you say will either acquit you or condemn you."

Perhaps, now you understand why it's important to watch what you talk about. Don't allow anyone to put words in your mouth. Some folks are good at that, but those same folks are often not good with God. Therefore, you decide your own speech so that you'll feel confident when it comes time to give an account. Speak well and you will be rewarded accordingly.

God bless you!

Sounds Weird, but It's True

From time to time, we read things in the Bible that sound weird—for instance, "Love your enemies." When I was a new believer, that sounded weird to me; I preferred an eye for an eye or tooth for a tooth. Little did I know of the many benefits that are attached to showing love for my enemies: peace, joy, being able to sleep through the night, and watching our God make the enemy our footstool. I've seen it happen several times.

Here's another weird saying that a new believer might notice in James 1:2–3: "Dear brothers and sisters, when troubles come your way, consider it an opportunity for great joy. For you know that when your faith is tested, your endurance has a chance to grow." The natural man would never put "troubles come your way" and "joy" in the same sentence. The Holy Spirit, however, sees things differently. It makes little sense to us because we cannot see the big picture. When we are filled with the Holy Spirit, then the Word of God will make perfect sense, and even if it sounds weird, we know He is true. Develop a solid plan of reading your Bible every day and watch your wisdom and understanding increase rapidly. We sin daily, that is why Jesus had to die for us. Sounds weird, but it's true.

God bless you!

Are You Alive or Just Making Excuses?

I know many people who waste time and energy by just hanging around, chatting and accomplishing nothing. Their failure to accept Jesus as Lord and Savior disqualifies them from real living. Only when we are alive in Christ does this life start to make sense. Many people are full of excuses and can give you a hundred reasons why they shouldn't follow Jesus right away—unaware that they are spiritually dead. There's nothing new there; same thing happened in Bible times. Luke 9:59–60 says: "He said to another person, 'Come, follow me.' The man agreed, but he said, 'Lord, first let me return home and bury my father.' But Jesus told him, 'Let the spiritually dead bury their own dead! Your duty is to go and preach about the Kingdom of God.'"

My friends, I can truthfully say that I didn't start enjoying life until I realized it was not about me. Selfish people still trying to find their way undergo many days of senseless misery. A word for those who are still making excuses: there are two types of people in the world—those who make things happen and those who watch things happen. Why not accept Jesus as Lord and Savior and start making some things happen. Come alive and give Him glory. Work for Him and watch Him bless you beyond measure.

God bless you!

Divided Highway

One thing is certain: a divided highway is two-directional. If one side is going east, the other goes west. If one side is going north, then the other goes south. The same is true for individuals who plan on making it to heaven but often switch to the other side of the highway. This is what the Bible says in James 4:8: "Come close to God, and God will come close to you. Wash your hands, you sinners; purify your hearts, for your loyalty is divided between God and the world."

Distractions are everywhere around us, so please let us be mindful of our activities. If we are not sure if a particular activity goes against God's will, then we need to pray and ask Him for clarity. Everyone has struggles, and that will always be a fact until we get to heaven. However, are we conquering or being conquered by our struggles? We are more than conquerors if we remain on the correct side of the highway. Let us purify our hearts and stay on the highway heading north to that glorious place called heaven. The highway to hell will always be there for those who choose that way, but the wise person will avoid that ride. Open your eyes wide and see the highway divide. Partner with Jesus, our Lord, and remain on the victorious side.

God bless you!

Velcro or Scarecrow?

Velcro is a brand that makes devices that stick together. Scarecrows are humanlike figures used to scare birds away from newly planted seeds. What's my point? When we, humans, separate ourselves from one another, we behave like scarecrows. Maybe someone did you wrong, and you can't find it in your heart to forgive. You become a scarecrow to defend the seeds in your heart. If you are in that position, please take a look at what the Bible says in Proverbs 17:9: "Love prospers when a fault is forgiven, but dwelling on it separates close friends."

When a fault is forgiven, we behave like Velcro adhesive. Love is evident, and unforgiveness is defeated. What a pleasant way to live where people aren't scared to get close to us. That will surely give us a more enjoyable life. Learn a lesson from this comparison. The more we behave as a scarecrow, the more we will look like one. Let's draw closer in love to one another and separate the evil mindset from our lives.

God bless you!

When Your Plans Are Evil, Don't Exclude You

People plan evil in their hearts daily. It's not difficult due to the fact that individuals do things that are not pleasing to us. We as believers, however, must stop those evil thoughts and plans before they escalate into something catastrophic.

Here's a prime example. In the Book of Esther, Mordecai refused to bow down and honor Haman. When Haman found out, he was furious, which led to his downfall. The Bible says this in Esther 3:5–6 and Esther 7:10: "When Haman saw that Mordecai would not bow down or show him respect, he was filled with rage. He had learned of Mordecai's nationality, so he decided it was not enough to lay hands on Mordecai alone. Instead, he looked for a way to destroy all the Jews throughout the entire empire of Xerxes. So they impaled Haman on the pole he had set up for Mordecai, and the king's anger subsided."

If you haven't read this story, now is a good time to check it out. The morale of it is this: don't plan evil for your neighbor, unless you include yourself as one of the recipients. Jesus says if we don't forgive, then our father in heaven won't forgive us. Plan good instead of evil, and the same will be true to you.

God bless you!

Real Faith versus Useless Faith

It takes faith to believe in God—that goes without saying. However, that faith alone is not enough to impress God. Anyone with a little common sense can figure that out. So, what type of actions constitutes real faith? The answer is simple: good deeds. Let's see what the Bible says regarding this in James 2:19–20: "You say you have faith, for you believe that there is one God. Good for you! Even the demons believe this, and they tremble in terror. How foolish! Can't you see that faith without good deeds is useless?"

Believing we have faith and not sharing the Gospel as well as not helping those in need whom God placed in our path and instructed us to help or worrying about things that God promised to fix in our lives are all useless faith. Let's exercise real faith in our lives, not lip service. Something to remember: "As the Lord leads, we follow with good deeds!" Help the poor and needy, be a listening ear to someone in distress, pray for the lost—the list goes on and on. We don't have to broadcast the good deeds we have done because God's video camera is always rolling. Soon you'll receive your reward, so don't grow weary in working hard. Your faith is established by your works, so work well.

God bless you!

The Alarm of the Righteous

When we're sleeping and the alarm goes off, we know it's time to wake up. If you're like me, you'll hit the snooze button once or twice before getting up. It may or may not be imperative for you to wake up early in the morning—that depends on what you have to do. However, it is imperative that we wake up and see what's happening around us. The Bible says this in Joel 2:1–2: "Sound the alarm in Jerusalem! Raise the battle cry on my holy mountain! Let everyone tremble in fear because the day of the Lord is upon us. It is a day of darkness and gloom, a day of thick clouds and deep blackness."

The righteous have plenty of work to do. We all know people who are sleeping spiritually. What are we doing to wake them up? By inviting them to church, you are sounding an alarm. By showing them love and kindness, you are sounding an alarm. By warning them in a firm but loving way, you are sounding an alarm. As with our home alarm clocks, we can either get up or stay in bed. Individuals who hear a righteous alarm can either accept salvation or stay dead. There are many Christians, ministries, and media outlets that sound alarms. Take off your headset and wake up.

God bless you!

Stop Rejecting and Start Accepting

Most people reject the Gospel message because rather than live for God, they are involved in what they believe is more important. They need to rearrange their priorities before time runs out. Others reject the Gospel message because they don't like the messenger. If you are a messenger of the Gospel and you keep getting rejected, don't quit; pray hard. They are rejecting not you but Jesus and God the Father. The Bible says this in Luke 10:16: "Then He said to His disciples, 'Anyone who accepts your message is also accepting me. And anyone who rejects you is rejecting me. And anyone who rejects me is rejecting God, who sent me.'"

My dear brothers and sisters in Christ, we need to pray hard for family members and friends who don't want to hear the Gospel. By rejecting your words, they are accepting the title Enemy of God. If you have not accepted Him and you're hearing this powerful declaration, I encourage you to accept Him today. Say, "Lord God, I repent of all my sins. Wash me clean and make me new. Thank you, Jesus, for dying on the cross for me and for being raised on the third day. I accept your salvation in Jesus's name. Amen!"

Welcome aboard, my friend! If you are still in the valley, stop rejecting and start accepting.

God bless you!

Sunrise to Sunset

We love the sunrise, don't we? We are able to look outside and see things clearly because the darkness has been overpowered by the sunlight. Now in some areas we can look at the sunset and see a beautiful display of God's awesome power. However, after the sunset is a cause for concern in some lifestyles. Many people fail to pay their spiritual power bill, and when the sunset comes about, they have no light from Christ—only darkness.

The Bible says this in Psalm 90:12: "Teach us to realize the brevity of life, so that we may grow in wisdom." When we realize that our time here on earth is only for a short time but that our time in the next life after our sun sets is for eternity, we would plan accordingly.

Not wanting to sound gloomy, I pray you would give this serious thought while your sun is still risen. Don't get caught in darkness thinking you had more time because unlike your local electricity provider, you won't be able pay and get reconnected once you're shut off. Our sunset is a mystery; no one has a set expiration date under normal circumstances. The wise person will then make preparations for heaven by repenting and having their sins forgiven. Enjoy the sunrise, but be ready for the sunset.

God bless you!

Get Off the Chair of Judgment

We hear it every day—one person judging another, coming to their own conclusion without even knowing all the facts.

It is time to get off the chair of judgment, my friends. The Bible plainly tells us this in James 4:11–12: "Don't speak evil against each other, dear brothers and sisters. If you criticize and judge each other, then you are criticizing and judging God's law. But your job is to obey the law, not to judge whether it applies to you. God alone, who gave the law, is the Judge. He alone has the power to save or to destroy. So what right do you have to judge your neighbor?"

We have no right because, quite frankly, we all have faults; no one is perfect. Let's focus on building others up rather than tear them down with gossiping friends. We have a choice each day—to use our mouth to bring glory either to God or to Satan. Stop judging, start loving, and watch the blessing that comes your way. Keep in mind that the righteous judge will judge our actions. Let's choose to obey Him.

God bless you!

Hold On to Your Crown

The crime rate on a global scale is at an all-time high. One area specifically is theft—people are stealing now more than ever. In an effort to protect ourselves from being robbed, we often place our valuables in safe deposit boxes and our money banks. Let me point out one thing that the master thief is stealing daily from many who believe Jesus Christ is Lord: he is stealing their crown.

Jesus warns us in Revelations 3:11: "I am coming soon. Hold on to what you have, so that no one will take away your crown."

The wise person will put more effort in securing an eternal crown versus a temporary one. Don't lose focus along the journey, my friends! This life is passing. What about the everlasting? Don't trade in your crown of righteousness for a crown of sinfulness. Put on the whole armor of God. Fight the enemy with confidence knowing that the victory is yours. The alternative is to do what Satan asks of you, lose your crown, and end up in hell. As for me, I'll choose option A and fight those evil spirits. I pray you do the same and keep your crown.

God bless you!

Live by the Manuscript

The Bible as we know it today was originally a manuscript. The definition of manuscript is: "A book or document written before the invention of printing." It also means: "The original handwritten text of an author's work." The reason why this is important is simply this: listening to a pastor or anyone else tell you about the Bible rather than read for yourself won't have the same effect. You need to read for yourself, hear the heart of Jesus, give your soul to him, and proclaim this Good News to someone else.

This is what the Bible says in Psalm 119:14–16: "I have rejoiced in your laws as much as in riches. I will study your commandments and reflect on your ways. I will delight in your decrees and not forget your word." Do we delight, study, and rejoice in God's manuscript? That is a question only you can answer. Keep in mind that if you say you love Jesus but don't truly love reading His Word, your love is conditional. Why? Because the Word is Jesus in written form. Think about this as you journey on your Christian walk. For those who are still not saved, it's time to wake up and voluntarily enter a good Bible-teaching church before you are carried in by six strong men. We either live by God's manuscript or Satan's.

God bless you!

Much-Needed Meditation

We meditate every day on various things; sometimes, things that hold no real value. Nonetheless, our minds are preoccupied by them. What about the spirit man? How much time do we spend meditating on God's love specifically to feed our spirit man? Please don't undermine the spirit man; he is your direct connection to your Creator and God.

The Bible says this in Psalm 48:9: "O God, we meditate on your unfailing love as we worship in your Temple." Going to church or the temple is great, but we need to meditate and worship daily in spirit and in truth. Make this a priority and pause for the cause. What can you expect from this much-needed meditation? For starters, God will reveal fresh revelations, not to mention you'll begin a closer walk. Once we've received these things and shared our experience, we'll help the lost to find their way.

This is what Jesus did. He got up early in the morning, spent time with God in meditation and prayer, and then went and ministered to the lost. You can ignore this if you want to, but just remember that by your fruits, they—both God and everyone around you—will know you. So meditate, be great, and elevate someone else's faith.

God bless you!

Raw Uncut Meat of the Word

There are too many diamond dealers in the pulpits. Let me explain. When a diamond is in the rough, part of the stone that won't shine is cut away. To form a diamond into a certain shape, it's cut, and, most times, good diamond is thrown away in the process. In churches today, many pastors dance around scriptures that are good for the soul but bad for popularity. This is what Jesus says in Matthew 23:15 to the teachers who deliver malnourished sermons: "What sorrow awaits you teachers of religious law and you Pharisees. Hypocrites! For you cross land and sea to make one convert, and then you turn that person into twice the child of hell you yourselves are!"

The Word of God is sharper than any two-edged sword, so we will get cut sometimes. Don't allow status to pull you away from the raw and uncut meat of the Word and have you on a "see food" diet. This means that whatever food you see that entices you, you eat it. The devil has many traps set, and only when the unadulterated Word is breathing through your lips and life will you successfully avoid them. Spiritually speaking, the Word of God is already seasoned, cooked, and ready to partake of. Don't add to it or take anything away. Eat Him raw.

God bless you!

Carefully Selected

Whether you are reading these words of encouragement or hearing them, you have a reason to be grateful to God. You were chosen to do great works for His Kingdom. God could have taken you home while still in your mother's womb, but He didn't. Statistics show that one in every four pregnancies in America end in miscarriage. That's approximately six hundred thousand a year!

On a global scale, we can't keep an account; there's just too many to count. How blessed we are to even be here in the first place. I am convinced that we were carefully selected by God to accomplish His will. This is what God told Jeremiah in Jeremiah 1:5: "I knew you before I formed you in your mother's womb. Before you were born I set you apart and appointed you as my prophet to the nations." Perhaps, your calling is a little different from Jeremiah's. How will you know exactly what you were selected for without being close to God, who does the selecting?

I urge anyone reading or listening to look into a right relationship with God. You are very special, my friend, regardless of what another individual may think of you. God has a purpose and a plan for your life that you were carefully selected to come to pass. He designed you for a task and will gladly instruct you, so just ask. Repent of your sins and get to know the King of Kings! You were carefully selected for that.

God bless you!

Lover of God or Liar?

The word *love* gets thrown around so loosely by mankind. Most people who use the word *love* have no idea of its real meaning. They don't realize that love is patient, kind, and not rude, just to name a few.

One of the biggest lies people tell is that they love God. I consulted the Bible with regard to that statement, and this is what the Bible says in 1 John 4:20–21: "If someone says, 'I love God,' but hates a Christian brother or sister, that person is a liar; for if we don't love people we can see, how can we love God, whom we cannot see? And He has given us this command: Those who love God must also love their Christian brothers and sisters."

There you have it, my friends. Love and hate for mankind cannot dwell in the same heart. Let's be forgiving and loving to all and stop lying to ourselves and others in saying that we love God. Work on truly loving your fellow man, and only then will our love for God be real. Some people make it hard for others to love them, and I know this is true, but think about how, despite everything wrong we've done unto God, He still loves us.

I encourage you today to pray. Ask God to point out any individual you find difficult to love and to give you the strength to love them. Don't dismiss this if you truly want to be a lover of God and not a liar. Loving people opens the door to loving God.

God bless you!

A Reason to Praise Him

Oftentimes, when I greet an individual by saying, "Praise the Lord!" they look at me and smile in a weird kind of a way. The correct response would be, "Yes, praise the Lord!" I have come to discover that many fail to praise the Lord, thinking they have no reason to do so. Well, for those with that mindset, allow me to give you a reason: you woke up this morning on top of your grave instead of in it. Once you have life, you have many opportunities available.

However, some things cannot be accomplished without Christ. This brings us to one of the reasons why we praise Him. Psalm 32:1 says, "Oh what joy for those whose disobedience is forgiven, whose sin is put out of sight!" Now, that is something to be joyful for. No one can bring their sinful ways to heaven, so trying to get to the Father without accepting the sacrifice Jesus made on the cross is a waste of time. My advice to you: begin a personal relationship with Jesus today. Get to know Him, and then you will truly know the Father. Once you are connected like that, AOL has nothing on you. Real Christians offer real praise without shame. Are you ashamed of His name? If not, praise His name to the ends of the earth.

God bless you!

We Can Boast About the True Believer

Self-praise is no recommendation, so don't do it. Allow someone else to boast about your serious walk with the Lord or your love for all mankind or your eagerness to forgive. It actually builds faith in the heart of the hearer when we boast about other believers. The Apostle Paul knew this and boasted about the church in Corinth. This is what he says in 2 Corinthians 7:13–14: "In addition to our own encouragement, we were especially delighted to see how happy Titus was about the way all of you welcomed him and set his mind at ease. I had told him how proud I was of you—and you didn't disappoint me. I have always told you the truth, and now my boasting to Titus has also proved true!"

What a blessing it is to see new believers keeping the faith in spite of all the challenges. We should boast about that. What about the seasoned believer struggling financially, physically, or emotionally but still stays true to God? We should boast about them too. Nonbelievers listen to us if we talk nonsense, so let's talk some sense into them with a different approach. Boast about the steadfastness of your Christian brothers and sisters. You will be planting a seed that prayerfully will take root and grow. Boasting you should do—just not when it's about you.

God bless you!

The One Who Truly Cares for You

A lot of us have gotten involved in relationships that ended in disappointment. Live and learn type deals. We've been disappointed when we were lied to by an individual who claimed he or she cared for us. Many fall into deep depression over similar circumstances and worry themselves to sickness.

Here is my take on this matter: God truly cares in spite of. The Bible tells us this in 1 Peter 5:7: "Give all your worries and cares to God, for He cares about you." There you have it, my friends. There is no need to worry, just give it to God and walk in His will. Don't attempt to force anyone to care for you; God cares for you. You may be the biggest sinner or a mature believer: God cares for you. Exercise some faith and that will be pleasing to him and then watch His rewards chase you down and overtake you. From time to time, a friend may say to us, "Who cares?" A good answer would be, "God cares!" Get the Word out. Shine your light for the one who truly cares for you. God sent His only begotten Son to die on the cross because He cares that much for the lost.

Now that we have established that God cares for you, the question is: do you care for Him? Live for Him and prove that you care for Him.

God bless you!

When the Role Is Called Up Yonder

Though not so popular among men today, there are some people—mainly believers—who look forward to heaven on a daily basis. We sing songs that encourage and put us in the mindset of heaven: "When I Get There," "Soon and Very Soon," and, "When the Role Is Called Up Yonder." What effect do these songs have on your heart? Do they cause you to think about heaven? Do you know what to expect when the role is called and your name is written in heaven? Here in Revelations 21:3–4, it gives us just a glimpse of something to look forward to: "I heard a loud shout from the throne, saying, 'Look, God's home is now among His people! God Himself will be with them. He will wipe away every tear from their eyes, and there will be no more death or sorrow or crying or pain. All these things are gone forever.'"

I am looking forward to that day. How about you? Are you ready for that day, or are you still in the spiritual dressing room? Be ready for glory, or accept what comes your way in a not-so pleasant lake of fire. Don't dismiss what you hear without doing your own research. Everyone will be called on that great day—some to eternal life and others to eternal punishment. Be encouraged. Get your house in order real soon so Jesus can reside with you.

God bless you!

There Is Something Better

Spiritual Growth is more than just a phrase; it's actually more important than physical growth. Our growth should be evident to others and not just ourselves. The problem most so-called believers have is a lack of true salvation. However, our lives will not be better without it on earth or in the next life. The Bible says this in Hebrews 6:7–9: "When the ground soaks up the falling rain and bears a good crop for the farmer, it has God's blessing. But if a field bears thorns and thistles, it is useless. The farmer will soon condemn that field and burn it. Dear Friends, even though we are talking this way, we really don't believe it applies to you. We are confident that you are meant for better things, things that come with salvation."

We need to revisit our salvation if we are not producing fruit. Let's prove to God and man that we are appreciative of our salvation, which is much better than anything or anyone we could ever get. Salvation is key to avoiding damnation. If you're on the wrong path or merely existing in a horrible lifestyle, there is change. Repent of your sins and accept Jesus as Lord and Savior, and I guarantee that there is nothing better. Don't stay on the outside and criticize. Come on in and enjoy Him.

God bless you!

We Die Daily So We Can Live

Death is not among the favorite topics to discuss. It takes our minds someplace we'd rather not go right now. However, another way to view death would be with regard to our flesh. While one death is mandatory, another would require us to volunteer. Some folks do, while most don't, because works of the flesh are easier to perform than those of a holy nature. For those who follow Christ, here's a reminder of why we die daily to flesh. The Bible says this in Romans 6:5: "Since we have been united with Him in His death, we will also be raised to life as He was."

Let's face it: the reason we sacrifice our flesh is so we will hear, "Well done, my good and faithful servant! Enter into my rest!" and not hear, "Depart from me. I never knew you!" You may doubt these things I am saying to you now, but look into the matter before totally dismissing it. There is no repentance in the grave. Everyone alive right now has the chance to stop evil and to do good. When this earthly life is over, there is no more chance to get right.

So, what will it be—die daily to flesh and live in the Spirit for your eternity with God, or live for your flesh now and be separated from God for all eternity? Though it's a no-brainer, it is still not understood by many. How about you?

God bless you!

Be Quick with the Ears and Slow with the Tongue

I wish people would stop blaming their peppery tongue on the spicy food they eat. Please remember: someone is listening to you.

For the nonbeliever, this is bad or not so bad, but for the Christian, it is downright embarrassing. As believers, we are instructed to study the Word to show ourselves approved. The Word of God says this in James 1:19: "Understand this, my dear brothers and sisters: You must all be quick to listen, slow to speak, and slow to get angry." Notice that the Word encourages us to listen before running our yappers. After all, God did give us two ears and one mouth as a reminder to listen at least twice as much as we talk. James also points out that we should be slow to get angry. Why? Well, anger fuels the negative fire that the tongue blazes.

Please control yourself in public and private situations. Remember that whatever we say cannot be taken back. We can apologize 'til thy kingdom come, but that individual will never forget what you said. Therefore, before you put your foot in your mouth, think about how your words will be received before talking. Jesus listened and then spoke on many occasions. So should we.

God bless you!

Watch Out!

The word *watch* can be used in many ways—for example, "What brand of watch are you wearing? Is it a Rolex or a Timex?" Let's carefully analyze how Jesus used the word *watch* in the following area of scripture. In Mark 13:35–37, Jesus says, "You too must keep watch! For you don't know when the master of the household will return—in the evening, at midnight, before dawn, or at daybreak. Don't let Him find you sleeping when He arrives without warning. I say to you what I say to everyone: Watch for Him!"

So my question to you, my friend, is this: do you watch for Him? Some are spiritually fast asleep yet believe they are watching. We should know for sure due to the importance of this matter. Our eternity depends on it. I've spoken to people who've done a hard time in prison—five, ten, twenty years—and it seemed like forever to them. Can you imagine forever isolated from God and living in torment? I am not trying to scare you; I just want to make you aware. Don't fall asleep spiritually, my friends. Watch out! The Bible tells us He is coming like a thief in the night for us who are awake and shining our lights. Watch out for Him.

God bless you!

Gifted to Help or Gifted to Brag?

There's been an ongoing debate regarding spiritual gifts, and many take them out of context. First of all, spiritual gifts are not learned; they are given to us by God. You cannot learn how to prophesy, how to heal someone, perform miracles, or speak in or interpret tongues. These are all gifts from God. The Bible says this in 1 Corinthians 12:7: "A spiritual gift is given to each of us so we can help each other."

Now, the big question: are we using our gifts to genuinely help someone or just to prove that we are super spiritual? It is time to give God the glory with the gift He has blessed us with. Stop bragging about giving someone wise advice because God gave you the words to say. Please look into the matter before using the gift God gave you. Make sure to use your gift to help and not to brag. Remember, Jesus is Almighty God, and in order to help us, He sacrificed His very life so that we can be saved. Surely we can sacrifice our ego, help someone, and at the same time give God the glory. We will all give an account for our actions, so do what's right.

God bless you!

Understanding True Abundance

Many people I've met from day to day are struggling in one area of life or another—for instance, the financially wealthy may have problems staying married, or the happily married are barely getting by financially. You see, God understands our struggles and He wants to bless us abundantly in the areas we are lacking in.

This is what the Bible says in Ephesians 3:20: "Now all glory to God, who is able, through his mighty power at work within us, to accomplish infinitely more than we might ask or think." If you haven't yet figured it out, having true abundance means having the Holy One of Israel, the Lord Jesus Christ, living within you. When we repent and accept His forgiveness, we become eligible to receive all His promises. Our puny little minds can't even imagine the vast fortune we have in Christ Jesus. While money might make you happy, only God gives real joy. Relationships may make you happy for a moment, but only God can give you a godly husband or a godly wife.

So, what will it be—a life separated from God or true abundance of peace? Throw in the towel on sinful living. If you do, let me be the first to welcome you to true abundance.

Congratulations and God bless!

A Not-So Popular Word

Church, in general, is supposed to be uplifting and encouraging. I am all for that. However, the church should be truthful and should teach the entire Bible. Everyone loves the promises of the Lord of blessings and prosperity, but what about the anger of the Lord regarding disobedience? Here is a not-so popular word taken from Lamentations 2:1: "The Lord in His anger has cast a shadow over beautiful Jerusalem. The fairest of Israel's cities lies in the dust, thrown down from the heights of Heaven. In His day of great anger, the Lord has shown no mercy even to His temple."

My encouragement to the church is simply this: turn from evil living and do good. Rid yourselves of sexual sin, lying, unforgiveness, and idolatry. Remember: one individual can stop the blessing of the church, just as Achan prevented Israel's blessing in Joshua 7. You've been lovingly warned to change your ways. No one knows in which capacity the Holy Spirit will bless, but I do know this: he will not bless a mess. Let's clean up our act and prevent the Lord's anger. His blessings are much nicer to receive. All scriptures are inspired by God.

God bless you!

When We All Get to Heaven

Some food for thought: not everyone who patronizes the airport flies away on an airplane. Likewise, not everyone who attends church services will be caught up in the rapture or make it into heaven at the time of their death. However, if an individual were to ensure that he has the necessary travel documents—true salvation—then they have no worries. Is making it to heaven your number one priority in this life? Please answer honestly because if your answer is no, then you are not ready yet.

Jesus says this in Mathew 13:45–46 (NLT): "Again, the Kingdom of Heaven is like a merchant on the lookout for choice pearls. When he discovered a pearl of great value, he sold everything he owned and bought it!" I am all for singing godly worship songs, but I am a bigger advocate for living out the godly worship songs. Analyze what Jesus is saying here: nothing should come before our place in Heaven. There's nothing wrong with having nice things on earth, but if they compromise our right standing in heaven, we don't need them. Let's be wise and really start planning for heaven. If we are not planning for heaven, then we are actually planning for hell.

God bless you!

CPSIA information can be obtained
at www.ICGtesting.com
Printed in the USA
FSHW01n1436020918
51895FS